JAZZ BIG BAND
for the Modern Drummer

by Ulysses Owens Jr.

PLAYBACK+
Speed • Pitch • Balance • Loop

To access audio, visit:
www.halleonard.com/mylibrary

Enter Code
1102-3552-6839-2661

ISBN 978-1-7051-7348-0

World headquarters, contact:
Hal Leonard
7777 West Bluemound Road
Milwaukee, WI 53213
Email: info@halleonard.com

In Europe, contact:
Hal Leonard Europe Limited
1 Red Place
London, W1K 6PL
Email: info@halleonardeurope.com

In Australia, contact:
Hal Leonard Australia Pty. Ltd.
4 Lentara Court
Cheltenham, Victoria, 3192 Australia
Email: info@halleonard.com.au

INTRODUCTION

On my first day of high school at Douglas Anderson School of the Arts, I was asked to audition for all of the jazz ensembles on campus. I had never formally played jazz before, but I figured I would give it a shot. I was then asked by my band director, Ace Martin, to play various grooves (samba, swing, funk, rock, shuffle, etc.), and the audition was done. A few days later, everyone ran up to me and told me to look at the board to notice that I not only got into jazz band, but I was selected for the top jazz band as a freshman, which was apparently unheard of. This began a fascination with the big band that was unique. Shortly after this wonderful experience, I spent four years in Jazz 1, and I was also selected for the All State, All District, and All County Jazz Big Bands. Time spent in these ensembles taught me a great deal as a student about what is necessary to know to successfully perform with a high school big band and even get accepted to college with a full scholarship to play jazz drums.

From the age of eight years old, I spent years playing for a 50–70 voice choir in the Pentecostal church, which I now realize was teaching me how to accompany the sounds that echo from a big band. Fast forward to now having my own big band, the Ulysses Owens Jr. Big Band, and we have recorded a successful debut record, *Soul Conversations*. The band was voted as the "Rising Star" in the big band category by *Downbeat* magazine in 2022. I have also been fortunate to tour and perform with the Count Basie Orchestra, John Beasley's Monk'estra, the Christian McBride Big Band, the Steven Feifke Big Band, Jazz at Lincoln Center Orchestra, the *Cotton Club Parade* (After Midnight) Broadway Big Band, and many other ensembles through the years. As an educator, nationally and globally, I have noticed that many drummers don't have a current reference of how to approach big band drumming in 2023, which merges with updated styles, charts, and multiple arranging perspectives.

This book will fully explore the history of big band drumming, styles, orchestration, and fills, along with effective ways to construct a drum solo. For those who already perform regularly with a big band, this book will also help improve existing skills and knowledge. Advice with regard to auditioning for high school and collegiate big bands is also offered here with multiple written examples and exercises. These exercises will assist in a proper introduction to the big band, or, for drummers with experience, it can even further their existing skills toward becoming a full industry professional.

This book is also a tribute to the great big band drummers past and present that very rarely get mentioned in the canon of great drummers, in my opinion. A band can only be as successful as the drummer, so I give major respect and love to the architects of jazz drumming, which began with big band drumming.

The Purpose of This Book

It really takes hands-on experience to truly learn how to play in a big band. This book is meant to help you gain the tools to do it, but actually doing it is imperative to really becoming a solid big band drummer. You must not only study this book; study must be accompanied by practice and consistency. Otherwise, this book will simply be a beautiful addition to your bookshelf.

Drum Legend

Part 1: What Is Big Band Drumming?

CHAPTER 1: What Is a Big Band?

A big band is a type of musical ensemble of jazz music that usually consists of ten or more musicians placed in four sections: saxophones, trombones, trumpets, and rhythm section. Some of the early big bands began as early as 1910, and one of the first bands was led by drummer Art Hickman in San Francisco around 1916. Other notable band leaders, such as Duke Ellington, played the Cotton Club in Harlem. Fletcher Henderson's band performed at the Roseland Ballroom, and there were other pioneering bandleaders of the big band sound, such as Paul Whiteman.

The swing era in 1930 sparked a huge emergence of big bands, which brought in groups led by Count Basie, Benny Goodman, Chick Webb, Jimmy Lunceford, and many other frontmen. There was a distinction between the hard-swinging bands like Count Basie and Tommy Dorsey, which played quick, hard-driving jump tunes, and "sweet/dance bands" like the Glenn Miller Orchestra, who performed more ballads and sentimental songs.

Jazz drumming begins with big bands, and for many drummers who never get the opportunity to play with a big band, there is a lack of maturity and musical experience that will be missing from your playing. To play with a big band is to accompany 16–17 horns with rhythm section, read music, and keep the groove simultaneously while kicking the hits with the arrangement. It's very challenging, and it's one of the first opportunities for drummers to take that journey from merely drumming to becoming a musician.

What Is Big Band Drumming for Me?

On my first day of high school, I got introduced to the sound of the big band via Jazz Band 1. However, I think the first chart I remember playing was probably a tune in 6/8 that kicked my butt. Then, I remember playing some Count Basie tunes, and, fortunately for me, my band director was great and knew how to shape a band.

As a young drummer, I spent many years playing funk, reggae, gospel, fusion, and small-group jazz stuff, but it wasn't until I took on the challenge of playing with a big band that I really began to develop as a musician. My ears opened up, and I began to understand why my technique had to improve because the music demanded it. However, I didn't learn until college that the pulse of a big band comes from the drummer, who is the conductor of the band, and the actual director essentially waves their hands for decoration. Ha!

Occupying the role of a big band drummer comes with a lot of responsibility; you must earnestly learn everyone's part to set them up musically in a tasteful way to play the chart. Big band drumming is very difficult for that reason; however, if you embrace the power and the responsibility, it can be an absolute joy. Being a big band drummer prepared me for producing and music directing because of the amount of information you have to be tuned to in real time.

However, as you dive into this book, understand there is no greater drumming honor than to kick a big band. This is because much of the evolution of jazz drumming began with drummers who were skilled in this genre of music.

How Does It Feel to Play with a Big Band to Me?

When you sit down on the drum throne, look to the left and see 15 horn players, then to the right and see the rhythm section there, and then you look out at the audience—there is no feeling like it.

I often tell people I was fortunate to grow up in a "pre-Pro Tools church," where I played for a choir every Sunday that consisted of 50–70 voices, which was daunting but so much fun. The big band is a scaled-down version of that, and you must adjust to all of the sounds, colors, and timbres that influence what you play.

Typically, as a drummer, our focus is connecting with the rhythm section, and that is what most drummers spend 90% of their career doing. However, I challenge you and every drummer to seek out opportunities that cause a change to your musical palette, pushing you to play differently.

Why Is This Still Relevant?

When I teach lessons in my private drum studio, I often ask potential students one important question: "Are you a drummer or a musician?" They often look at me with a perplexed look and I laugh, so I will pose the question again to you, the reader:

"Are you a drummer or a musician?"

I have a simple answer: If you have never played with a big band, singer, or anything out of the context that forces you to deal with orchestration and phrasing, then, unfortunately, you have just been a drummer. After studying this book and seeking big band opportunities, you will successfully take the journey of becoming a musician, which sets you apart from other drummers and creates a distinction, setting you on the path of mastery.

Part 2: Command of Your Instrument

The most important thing in big band drumming is the ability to control the sound of the drum kit with your technique and facility, because if you are unable to, then it will be challenging to power the band, set up fills, and get through a big band chart successfully.

CHAPTER 2: Necessary Techniques to Command Your Instrument

Fifty percent of the challenges that most drummers have with big band playing is a product of their technique. The issues that arise are because not enough practice focuses on building technique and eliminating technical weaknesses. This section is going to test your technique and facility to make sure that you are able to play the drums with the right amount of technical prowess and independence. It's important to make sure that you have the necessary chops to power through a big band and play the necessary fills required. To test your hands and the fluidity that you have, I have created a few exams.

Rudiment Exam

This exam will focus on your ability to play four rudiments at various tempos. Play each exercise for 60 seconds without stopping. If you get through the whole set, move on to the next level. If you're unable to make it through all of them, keep practicing these as you work your way through the book. Focus on your ability to play these with ease. As you master them, add in other rudiments and practice them in a similar way to create an effective warm-up routine.

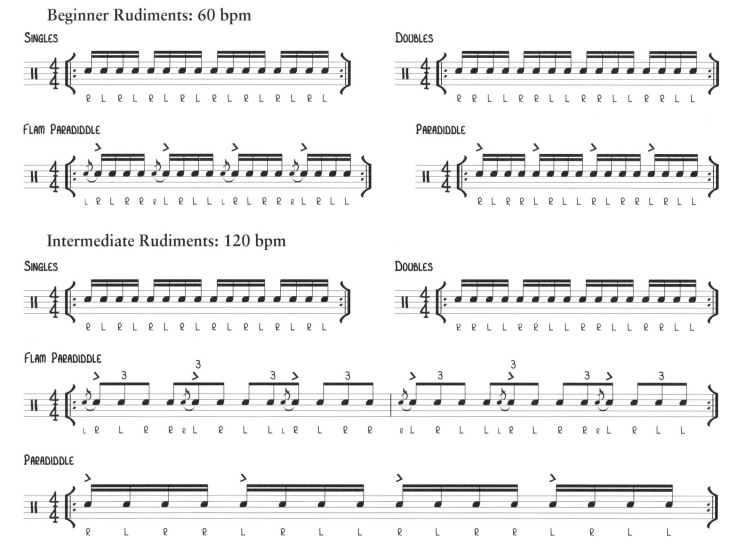

Experienced Rudiments: 160 bpm

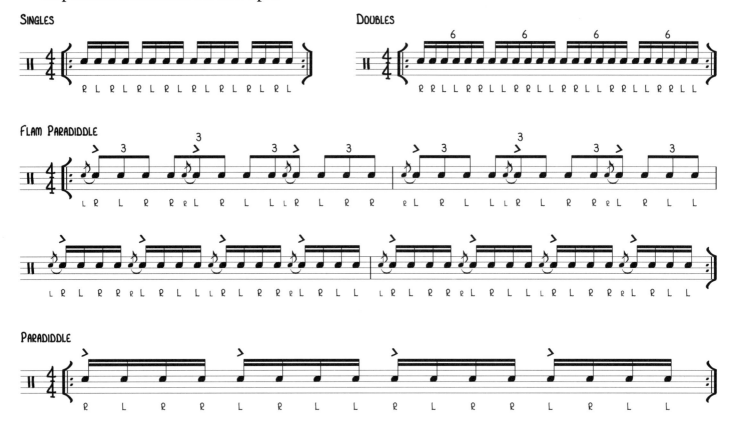

SINGLES

RLRLRLRLRLRLRLRL

DOUBLES

RRLLRRLLRRLLRRLLRRLLRRLL

FLAM PARADIDDLE

L R L R RrL R L LlR L R RrL R L
L R L R RrL R L LlR L R RrL R L

L R L R RrL R L LlR L R RrL R L L   L R L R RrL R L LlR L R RrL R L L

PARADIDDLE

R L R L R L L L R L R L R L L L

Groove Exam

This exam will focus on your ability to play some common grooves used in big band charts at various tempos. It is essential that you have a strong command of these feels so you can support the band by keeping the groove solid and playing what's needed.

Many charts only give the name of a groove, so it's up to the drummer to understand what to actually play. Study as many styles as you can so you'll have the confidence to play anything you might encounter. Play each groove at the indicated tempo for one to two minutes. If you're unable to play the tempo, then slow it down, master the beat, and work your way up to tempo. It's better to master something slowly before going for speed. As you master these, explore other tempos, both slower and faster.

Beginner Grooves: Funk, Swing, Afro-Cuban, Shuffle

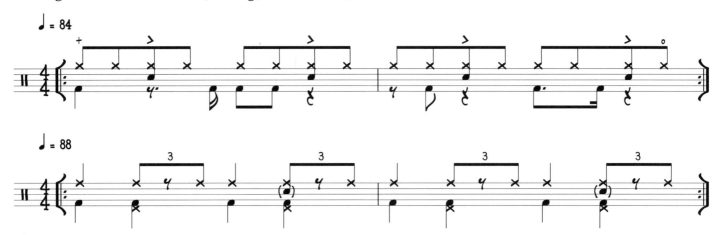

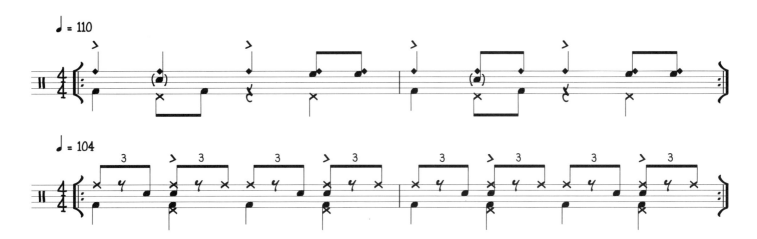

Intermediate Grooves: Funk, Swing, Afro-Cuban, Shuffle, 3/4 Swing, Jazz Ballad with Brushes

(For the second example, play it two times through as written and then two times in a double-time feel.)

*RIDE, BELL OF RIDE, OR SIDE OF SHELL (CASCARA PATTERN)

W/ BRUSHES

Experienced Grooves: Funk, Swing, Afro-Cuban, Shuffle, 3/4 Swing, 3/4 Swing with Brushes, 5/4 Swing

Independence Exam

This exam will focus on your ability to groove in various styles while reading rhythms. Try to stay relaxed and focus on keeping the groove locked in while playing the rhythms. If you find some that are difficult, slow them down and work them out so they feel easy and you understand the placement of the rhythm.

This method of reading and playing is a common way jazz drummers build coordination and vocabulary on the kit. Make sure to also spend time improvising with similar grooves and rhythmic motifs. You need to be a strong reader to navigate charts, but if you internalize these exercises, they'll also help with your fills, soloing, and overall groove. For all exams, play each repeated section four to eight times before moving on.

Beginner Independence: Swing, Bossa Nova

For the swing exercises, play a jazz ride cymbal pattern with hi-hat on beats 2 and 4 (as shown in A below), and add the rhythms as written from the subsequent snare and bass drum lines. Start off with a bpm of 88.

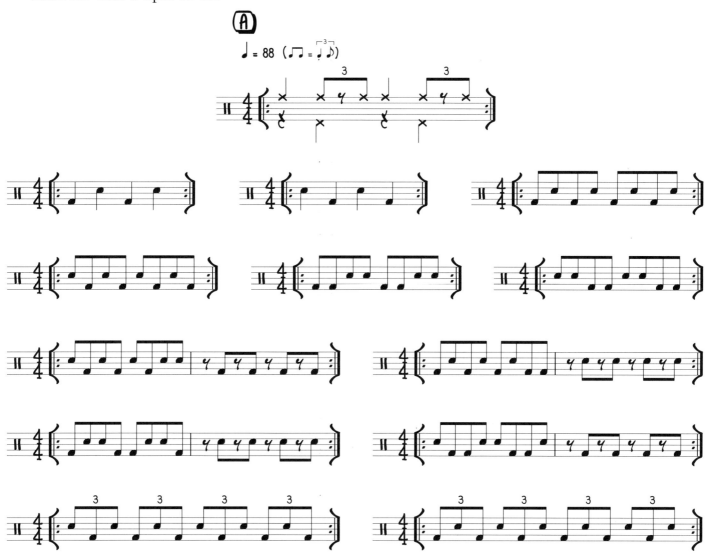

For the following bossa nova exercises, first play rhythms on the snare, alternating your hands while playing a samba foot pattern (A). Next, play the groove as a bossa nova, adding an eighth-note ride cymbal pattern (B). Play the rhythms on the snare line as a cross-stick or regular snare sound. Start off with a bpm of 90.

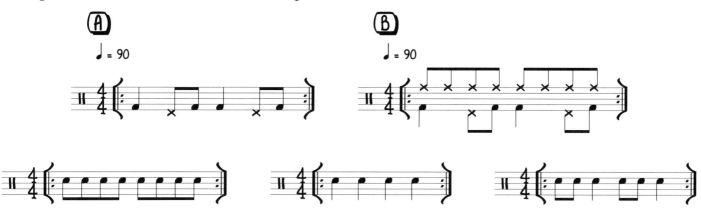

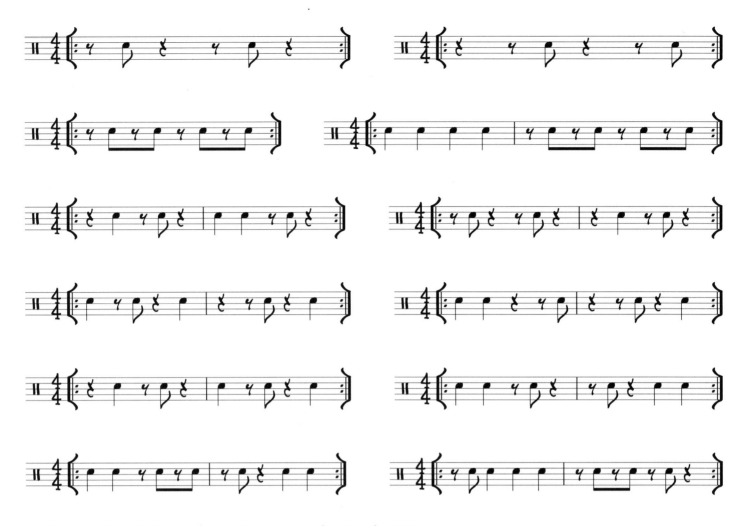

Intermediate Independence: Swing, Samba, Funk, 3/4 Swing

Play a jazz ride cymbal pattern with hi-hat on beats 2 and 4 (A), and add the rhythms as written from the subsequent snare and bass drum lines. Start off with a bpm of 120.

First, play the rhythms on snare, alternating your hands while playing a samba foot pattern (A). Next, play the groove as a fast samba, adding the ride cymbal pattern (B) while reading the rhythms from the snare drum lines below. Start at a bpm of 160.

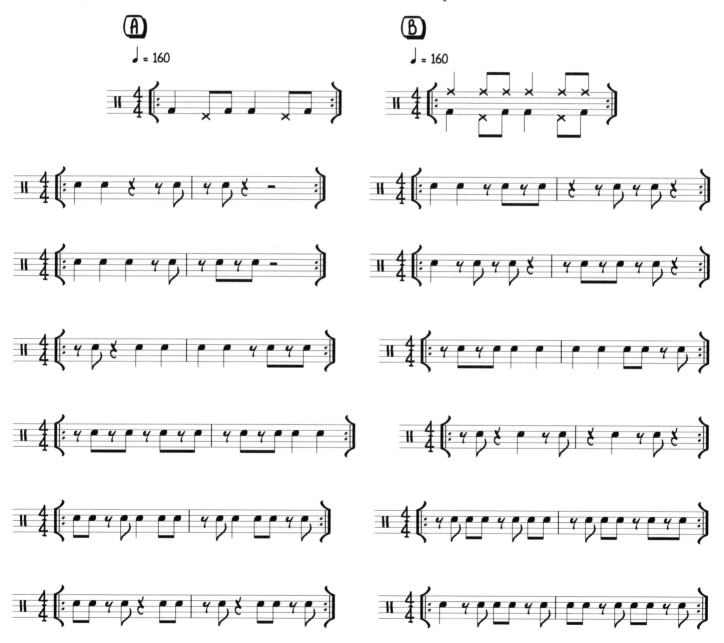

Next, play the groove with either eighth (A) or 16th (B) notes on the hi-hat with snare drum on beats 2 and 4 while also reading rhythms below in the bass drum. Sixteenth notes are less common than eighth and quarter notes, but they show up in charts, especially in rock and funk styles. Make sure you work on them so they don't trip you up. Start off at a bpm of 88.

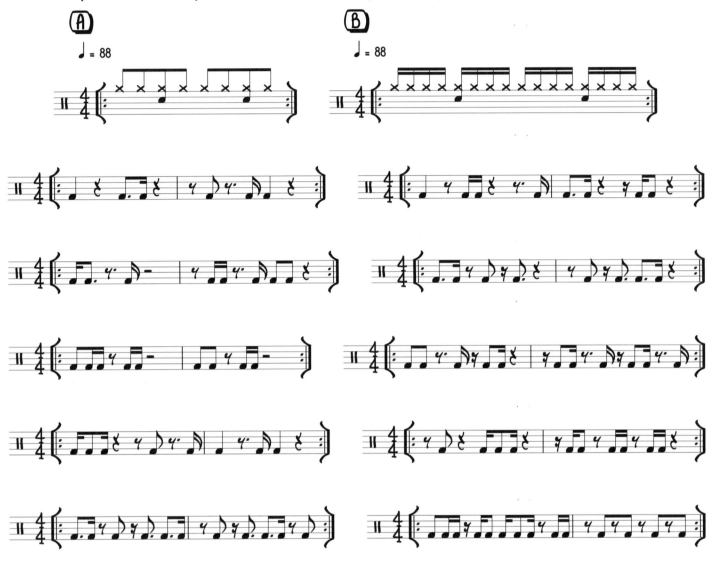

Play a 3/4 jazz ride cymbal pattern (jazz waltz) with hi-hat on beat 2 or beats 2 and 3 (A), and add the rhythms as written for snare and bass drum. Start off at a bpm of 90.

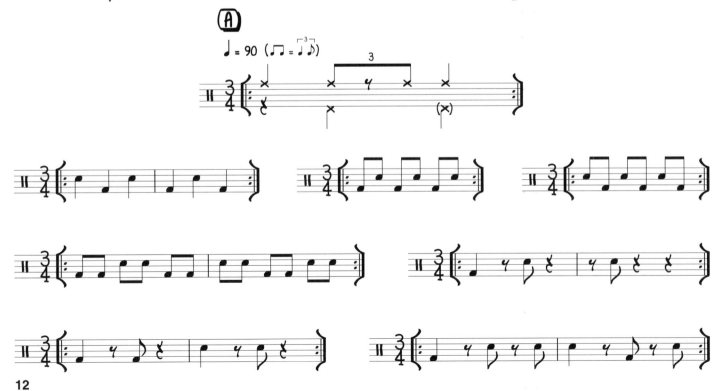

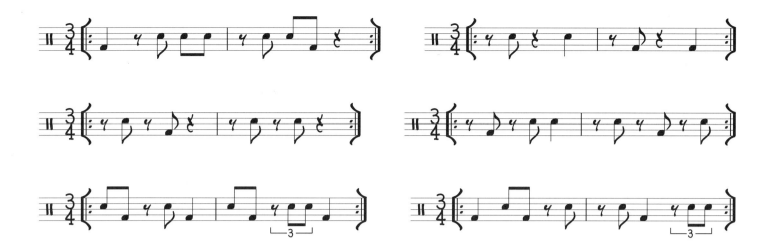

Advanced Independence: Swing, Samba, Afro-Cuban, Afro-Cuban 6/8, 5/4 Swing

Play a jazz ride cymbal pattern with the hi-hat on beats 2 and 4 (A), and add the rhythms as written from the snare and bass drum lines. Start at a bpm of 160.

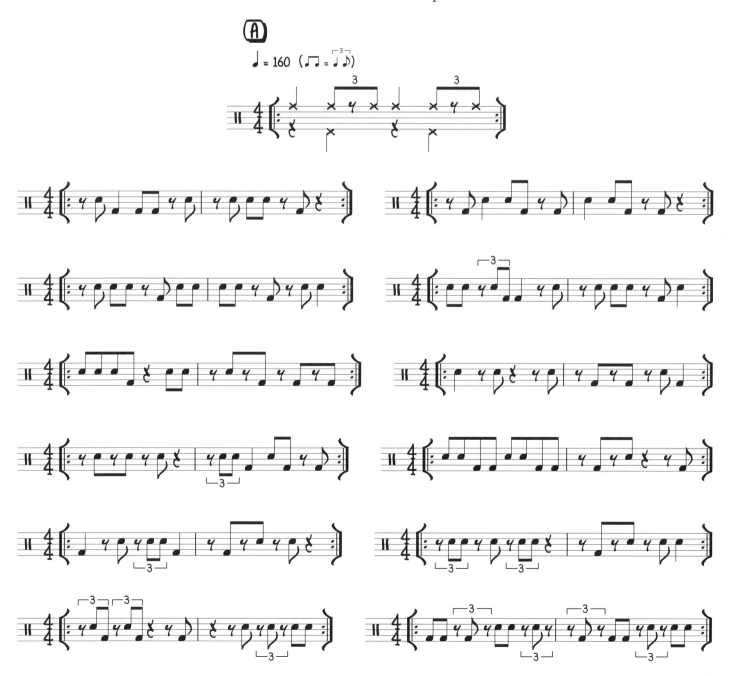

Try these next examples at 200 bpm.

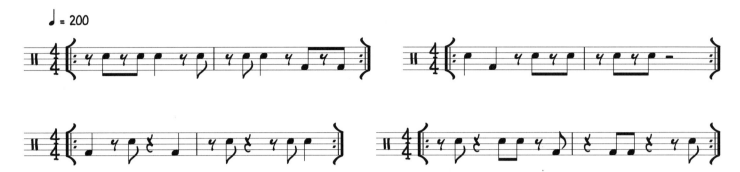

First, play the rhythms on snare, alternating your hands while playing a samba foot pattern (A). Next, play the groove as a samba, adding the ride cymbal pattern (B) while reading the rhythms in the snare drum line. 2/4 is another common way of writing a samba. Sometimes, it's written in 4/4 but using 16th notes. It's important to be fluid in reading all subdivisions. Start off with a bpm of 80.

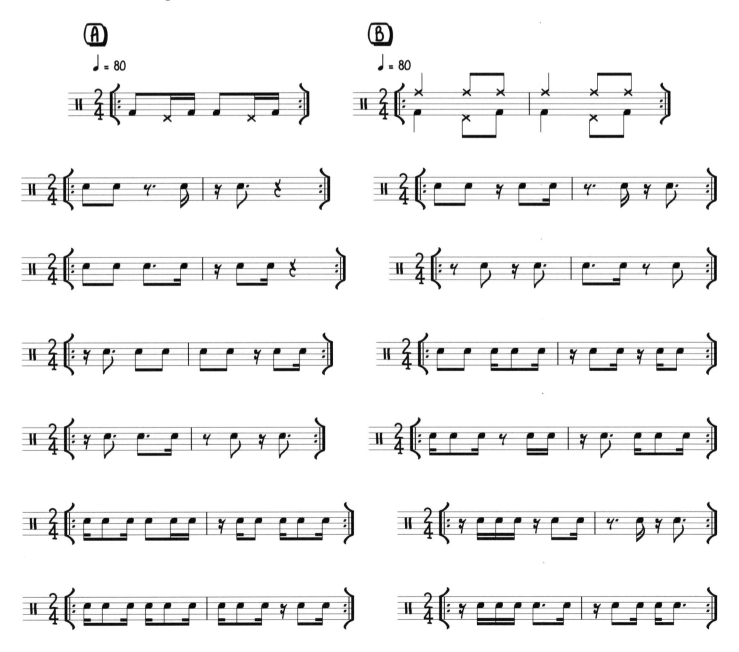

Play the hi-hat with your foot on beats 1 and 3 with the bass drum on the "and" of beat 2 and down on beat 4 (A). This bass drum pattern is often played by bass players in some Afro-Cuban styles and is referred to as *tumbao*. Add the written rhythms in the snare, alternating your hands. Start off at a bpm of 116.

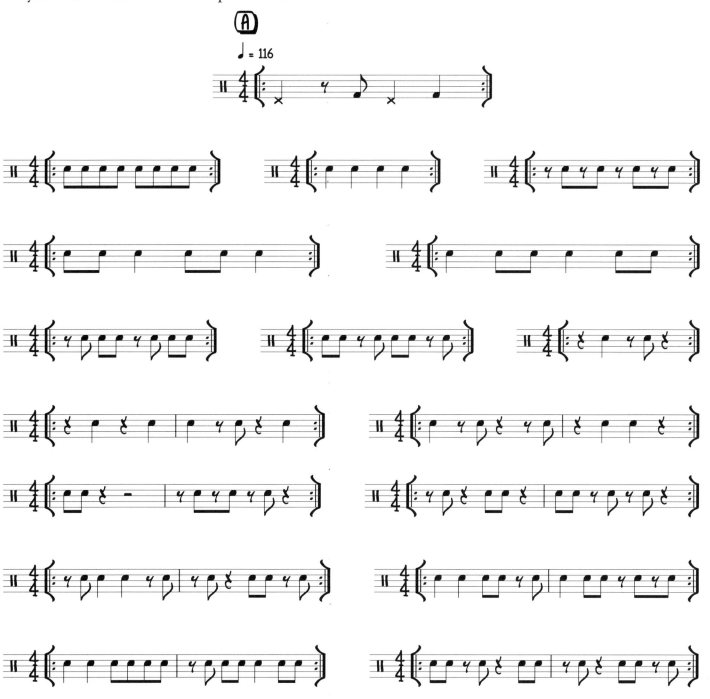

Play the ride cymbal on the bell for the written cymbal pattern (A). This is a common bell pattern for a 6/8 Afro-Cuban feel. Your feet play unison in a dotted quarter-note pulse. Add rhythms from the subsequent snare lines. Start off at a bpm of 80.

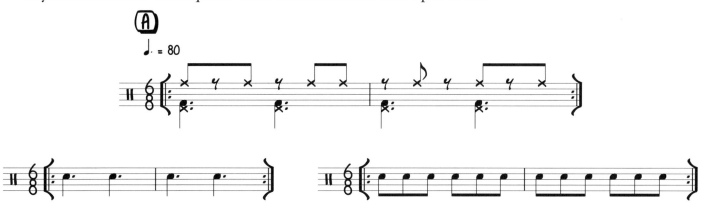

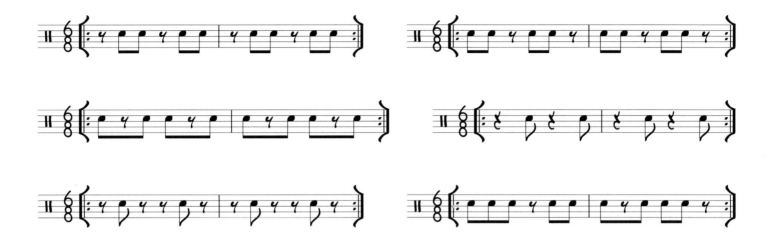

Play this 5/4 jazz ride cymbal pattern with the hi-hat on beats 2, 3, and 5. Add the rhythms as written from the snare and bass drum lines.

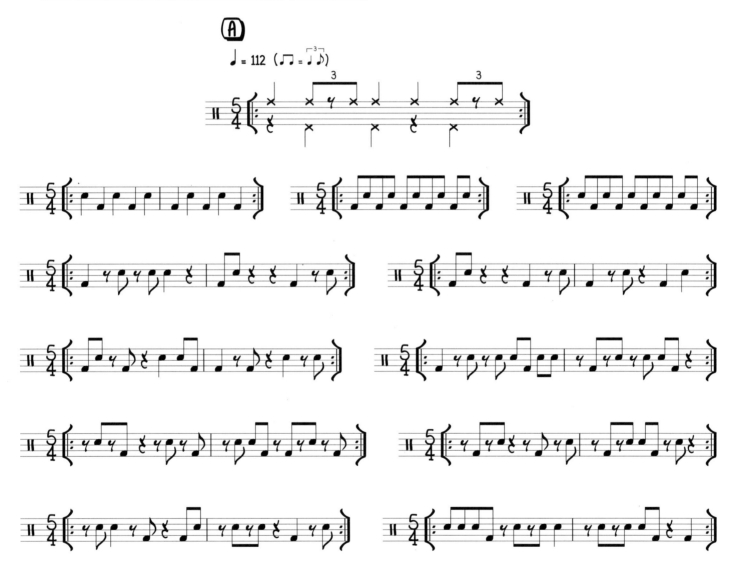

CHAPTER 3: Standard Big Band Grooves to Learn

A major part of effective big band drumming is learning to play the groove in a strong, impactful way that allows 16–17 members to feel the power of the drums and help them individually and collectively play the chart at hand.

In high school, my band performed a variety of swing, Latin, funk, rock, and New Orleans-style charts at a range of various tempos. Most referenced grooves of big bands from the 1960s through the 1990s. However, things changed when I was accepted to the Juilliard School's inaugural jazz department under the direction of Victor Goines, who is now the executive director at Jazz St. Louis and holds the second tenor chair in the Jazz at Lincoln Center Orchestra with Wynton Marsalis. Much of the big band repertoire that JALC performed was given to our band to study and perform. This was a challenge because, all of sudden, I had to study all of the great big band drummers: Mel Lewis, Herlin Riley, and Sonny Payne, among many others.

Here are some exercises highlighting standard grooves that most jazz big bands perform within the US in high schools, colleges, and professional ensembles. Later in the book, there is a chapter covering more modern grooves that are more current. It's important to learn all these grooves.

Standard Big Band Grooves

Swing

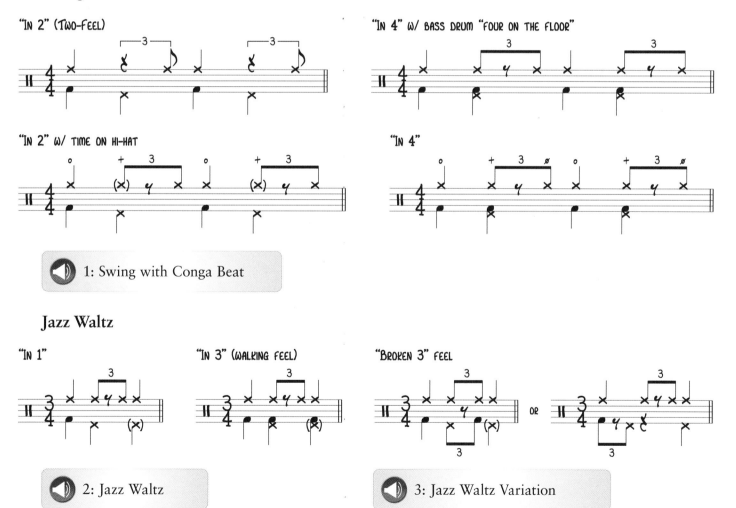

Jazz Waltz

Afro-Cuban

CASCARA W/ 2-3 SON CLAVE

CASCARA W/ 3-2 SON CLAVE

MAMBO (BELL OF RIDE OR COWBELL)

MAMBO W/ 2-3 SON CLAVE

 4: 4/4 Afro-Cuban Mambo Variation

Shuffle

5: Shuffle Variation

Ballad

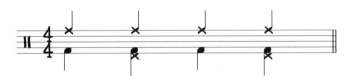

W/ BRUSHES

6: Walking Ballad with Sticks

7: Ballad with Brushes Variation

CHAPTER 4: Modern Big Band Grooves to Learn

The distinction must be made between standard drumset grooves that originated from the early 1900s and those that were played through the 1970s and '80s. However, within the last few decades, there has been a more modern approach to big band chart writing that is not solely anchored in 4/4 or swing. It extends to global grooves and multiple time signatures, requiring a broader understanding of playing grooves.

It's important to become aware of these modern grooves and how the forms of the tunes can be altered, so the same approach you would have on a Basie/Ellington-style chart is not applied to someone like Miho Hazama or an arranger influenced by Maria Schneider or Jim McNeely.

In many of the high school charts that I have read recently, I noticed a lot of different styles of rock and funk in addition to older-style charts. Bands like Gordon Goodwin's Big Phat Band and many others are worth checking out because of the kind of grooves that are required to play their charts correctly.

As with all the grooves presented here, these are just some variations—a good starting point. To really grasp a style and have command of the groove, you must listen and study masters of the genre. Grooves written down don't often relay how the groove really feels. Sometimes, charts are written by composers that have no idea of what the drummer should actually play. Other times, they want you to play something very specific that might not be something a drummer would normally play. By studying lots of grooves and styles, you can be ready to adapt to any circumstance.

Funk/Rock

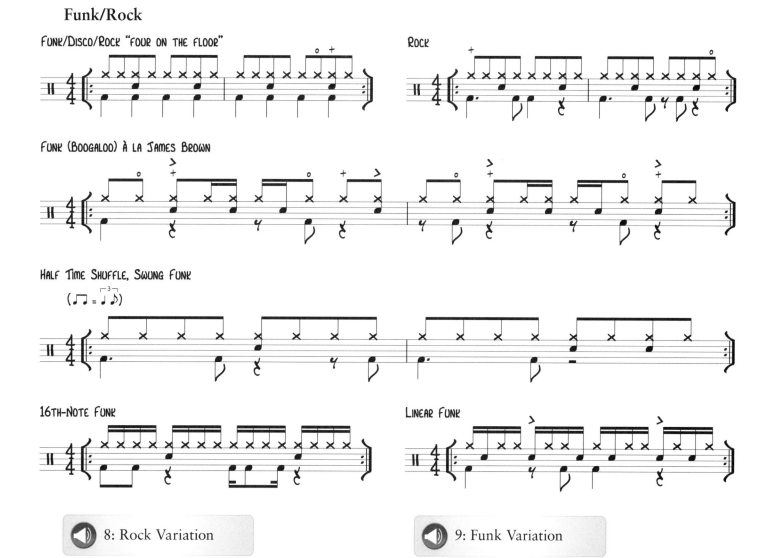

8: Rock Variation

9: Funk Variation

Afro-Cuban

Songo (play on ride or bell)

Songo w/ toms

Afro-Cuban 6/8

Afro-Cuban 6/8 (funk)

10: 4/4 Afro-Cuban Songo

11: 6/8 Afro-Cuban

Brazilian

Bossa Nova

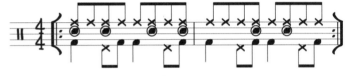

12: Bossa Nova Variation

13: Bossa Nova with One Brush & One Stick

Samba w/ Partida Alto (cross-stick or regular)

Samba w/ bell

14: Uptempo Samba

15: Uptempo Samba Variation

New Orleans

Street Beat/Second Line (play "in the cracks")

16: Second Line Variation

"Poinciana"

w/ mallets
snares off

Dixieland (both hands on snare)

17: Poinciana Variation

18: Dixieland Variation

Straight Eighth

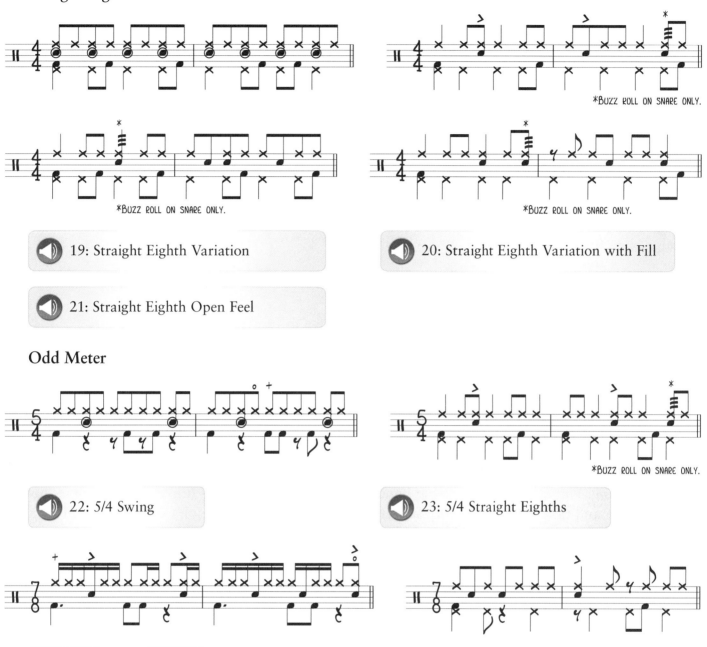

*BUZZ ROLL ON SNARE ONLY.

*BUZZ ROLL ON SNARE ONLY.

*BUZZ ROLL ON SNARE ONLY.

🔊 19: Straight Eighth Variation

🔊 20: Straight Eighth Variation with Fill

🔊 21: Straight Eighth Open Feel

Odd Meter

*BUZZ ROLL ON SNARE ONLY.

🔊 22: 5/4 Swing

🔊 23: 5/4 Straight Eighths

🔊 24: 7/8 Groove

Part 3: Kicking the Band—Set-Ups, Fills, and Soloing

The chapters within this section will explore the power of kicking the band with the right fills and set-ups. We'll also cover how to approach soloing with the big band in a substantial way that is best for the band and the chart.

It's important to notate the difference between "kicking" the band, "setting up" the band, playing the appropriate fills within the band, and soloing. All these aspects of playing with a big band have varying differences, and being aware of them will aid you in giving the band what they fully need.

- **Kicking the Band:** When it's time to power through a chart and the syncopated figures that are written within your part.

- **Setting up the Band:** When there is a figure (for example, on beat 4) within the music, you should be playing something on beats 1, 2, and 3 to help set up the band to play that figure.

- **Playing a Fill:** A fill will be necessary in a chart when you see rhythm slashes with the word "fill" above it, which means to play something rudimental to fill in that space within the chart. Within the big band, this is so important because often, if you don't play a fill, a big space will appear in the music and everyone will look at the drummer.

- **Soloing:** Playing a solo in the big band will be required, and it's important to utilize this space and take the opportunity seriously because again, if you don't solo, there will be a bunch of space. It won't look or sound good to the band or the audience.

CHAPTER 5: Combo vs. Big Band Playing

What Is the Difference?

Combo playing allows for more rhythmic freedom, and big band playing requires more discipline. Many times, drummers create major challenges with their big band approach simply because they won't accept the reality that one size does not fit all with combo and big band playing. There is a mental shift that one needs to make to play and support a big band, and that's often the first mistake that many young drummers make across the board.

Consider a new perspective, new gear approach, and a different focus on how the melody and groove is approached. This was one of the greatest lessons for me that finally clicked in college, that I had to learn how to have two different approaches on the drumset for small group versus big band. It's kind of like being Clark Kent or Superman, and I'll tell you: the big band needs Superman or Superwoman.

Combo Playing

You can take a groove and focus solely on it while playing around the melody, or you can play accented parts of it that you deem appropriate. Also, within combo playing, it's much more about your individual expression and less about a standard musical approach. Regarding gear, you can virtually use any kind of cymbals and drums you desire because the goal is your individuality within the music. (Example given on the following page.)

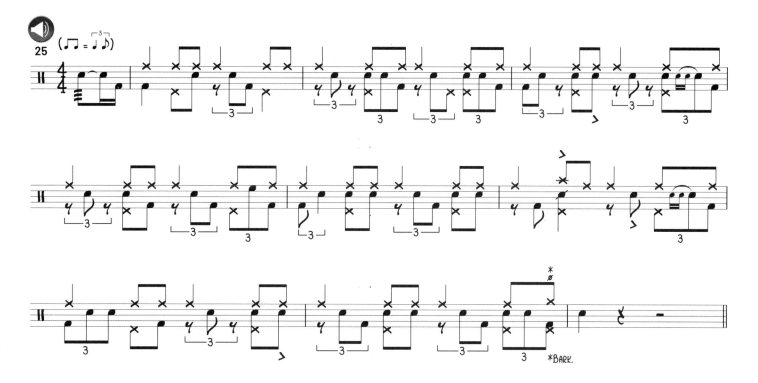

Big Band

I remember being in a recording session with the great Christian McBride Big Band for our Grammy award-winning album *The Good Feeling*. We were in the middle of a recording take, and I played a really busy fill on "Shake 'n Blake." McBride stopped the session and said, "Hey man, you got 17 mouths to feed; give us meat and potatoes!" This spoke to the simplicity that was lacking in my approach to the fills. I would extend this statement to grooving, phrasing, gear, and anything related to big band playing that I have described in this book.

Keep it simple because every decision you make as a big band drummer affects the band, which means everything you do is heard and noticed. It's essentially akin to being a parent versus being single. When you are single, you can do as you please; as a parent, your decisions affect your children. Think with a collaborative and responsible mindset, not an individual one. Remember: It's not about you; it's about the band.

Chopping Wood

There are several musical devices that drummers can utilize to anchor the band and assist them within a chart. The cross-stick is a great tool to rhythmically focus the band and keep everything on track musically. I remember when I was at Juilliard, Victor Goines would always tell me to "chop wood" with the cross-stick. You can use it on different beats, and it helps the band to focus and hear exactly where the groove is.

Chopping on 2

Chopping on 4

Chopping on 2 & 4

Backbeats

Backbeats are very important in the Basie/Ellington idiom of charts, so it's important to become familiar with how to utilize them.

Backbeat on 2 & 4

Set-Ups

Quarter Note Set-Up

*FEATHER BASS DRUM LIGHTLY.

Triplet Set-Up

*FEATHER BASS DRUM LIGHTLY.

16th-Note Set-Up

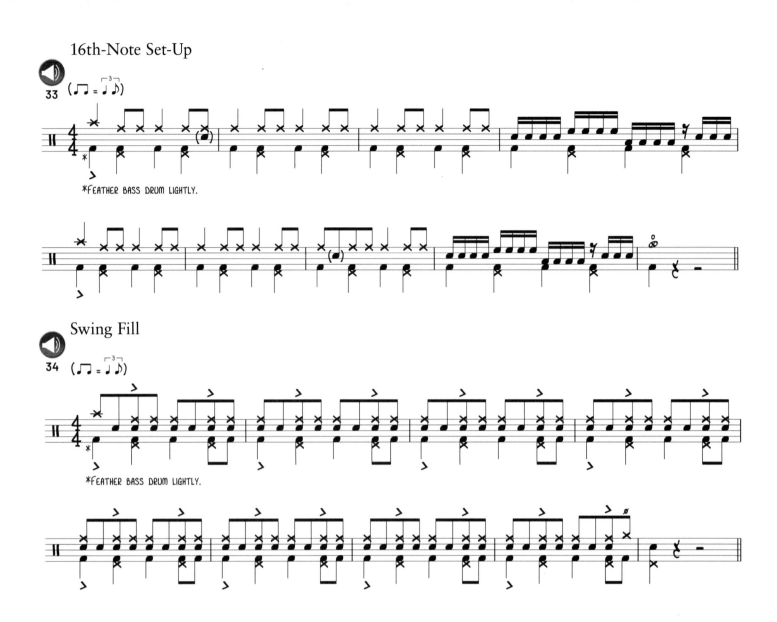

*FEATHER BASS DRUM LIGHTLY.

Swing Fill

*FEATHER BASS DRUM LIGHTLY.

Kicking the Band

All the previous sections are essential to learn, but one of the most important aspects of big band drumming is to learn how to "kick" the band, or in other terms, play the figures that are written within the part that connect with the brass and saxophones. Below are some exercises that can help you with starting the process of learning how to play figures with a big band. What's important is to keep the swing going in the ride cymbal with the hi-hat while playing these figures between the snare and bass drum.

Kicks on the "+" of Beat 1

Kicks on the "+" of Beat 2

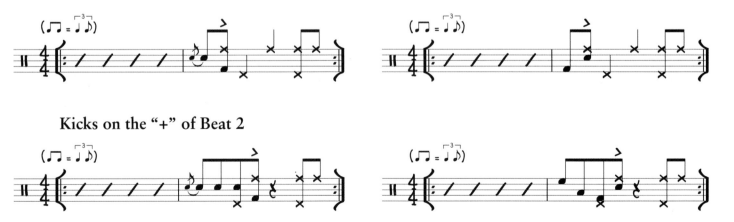

Kicks on the "+" of Beat 3

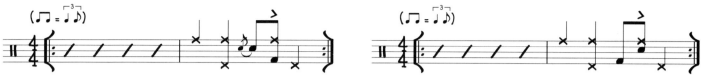

Kicks on the "+" of Beat 4

Kicks on Beat 1

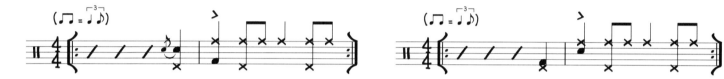

Kicks on Beat 2

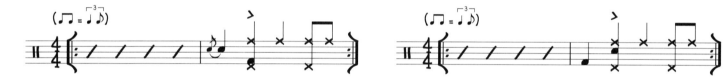

Kicks on Beat 3

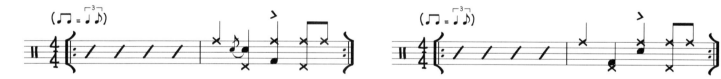

Kicks on Beat 4

CHAPTER 6: Big Band Fills to Learn

Standard Big Band Fills

An important element of big band drumming is the fill, which is a one-, two-, or four-bar set of solo ideas that propel the band into the next section of a tune. These fills are very key in telling the band when to enter a section, and they must be comprised of the right musical information.

In college, I remember spending hours studying Sonny Payne, Mel Lewis, Sonny Greer, Shadow Wilson, and so many other great big band drummers and the personality differences within their fills on each given arrangement. This is how I gained my vocabulary of options to play with each tune. The examples below demonstrate various fills that are foundational for my playing with a big band, and they are great resources for various styles of charts that each drummer reading this book will play.

Fills with Snare

The snare drum is a great starting point for fills especially if you are still building your comfort and technique; a lot of your feels can begin there, and it's musically sufficient for the band.

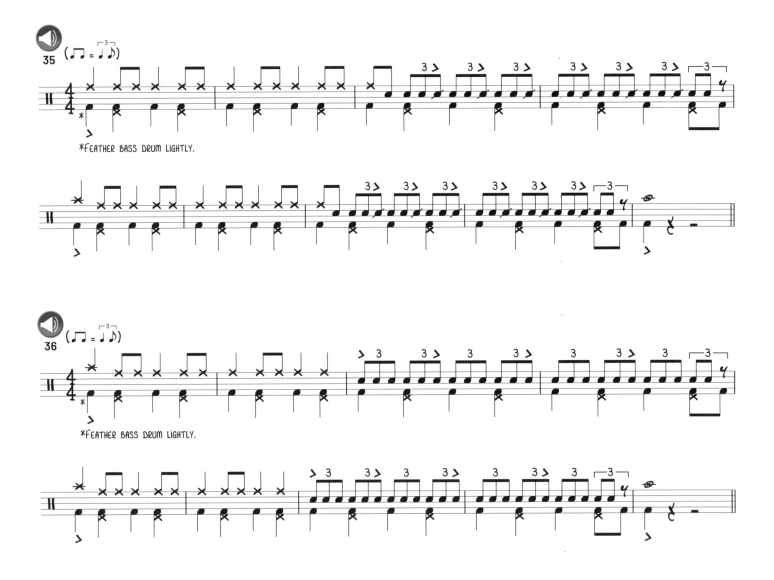

Fills with Toms and Cymbals

*FEATHER BASS DRUM LIGHTLY.

*FEATHER BASS DRUM LIGHTLY.

*FEATHER BASS DRUM LIGHTLY.

Fills with Full Kit

Fill Placement/Phrasing
Swing

Latin

Funk

3/4 Waltz

Afro-Cuban

Shuffle

5/4

CHAPTER 7: Soloing in the Big Band

In my opinion, some of the greatest drum solos happen within the context of big band. One of the key points is not only using your imagination but also pulling from information you have transcribed from great players. To learn how to solo, I feel it's important to approach it in segments of two bars and four bars. When considering longer phrases, you can still think about soloing within these groupings of bars.

Where to Solo?

Drum Shout Sections

Drum shout sections are essentially extended bars of solos, so if you can get comfortable with playing four, eight, or 12 bars, then this won't be an issue for you.

Open Drum Solo

This is probably one of the hardest solos to play because if you don't have any vocabulary, it's equivalent to someone dropping you off in a foreign country and telling you to have fun speaking the language with the locals. The reality is that if you don't have a vocabulary, you will be unable to speak the language.

Ways to Build a Drum Solo Vocabulary

Below are several ways to build your drum solo vocabulary, referencing the playing of other drummers, the melody, and channeling your confidence and creativity to tell a compelling musical story with unending ideas.

1. **Transcriptions:** This involves taking the time to transcribe the solos of the great drum masters by either creating written transcriptions or oral transcriptions—which is what I prefer.

   › Written transcription involves transcribing notes and rhythms by writing each idea on manuscript paper or utilizing notation software.

   › Oral transcription involves listening to the solo repetitiously and memorizing it. This works better for me because once I do that, the ideas remain in my playing forever.

2. **Use the Melody:** Within every jazz tune is a melody statement, and if you can't think of anything else to play, lean on the melody. If you just restate that rhythmically, it will give you some great ideas to start with and develop from there.

3. **Keep the Flow of Ideas Happening:** When you start playing a solo, *don't stop the music*! Often, young drummers become so intimidated by the idea of soloing that they don't just keep the ideas flowing consistently. This means you are doomed from the beginning.

4. **Play with Confidence:** Whatever you are able to do, do it confidently. If you aren't confident, it will signal to the band and audience that you don't know what you are doing.

5. **Tell a Story:** I speak about this in another book of mine, *Jazz Brushes for the Modern Drummer* (Hal Leonard). I view drum solos like an arc; I start with an opening statement, then I create a path to the middle, and then finally move to the climax.

Below, I play some examples of ideas that I enjoy utilizing with respect to the chart that I am playing. These examples also give the band what is necessary to nail entrances and have the right kind of energy.

Swing

FEATHER BASS DRUM LIGHTLY.

Latin

Funk

*Buzz roll on snare only.

**Bark.

3/4 Waltz

*Afro-Cuban

*Rim click.

**Bark.

The best way to get better at soloing is to practice. I want you to take the metronome, set it to 100 bpm, and play solos within four, eight, or 12 bars.

65: Bonus Solo

Part 4: Listening, Understanding, and Playing the Chart

Listening, understanding, and playing the big band chart is integral for the drummer because it addresses the intellectual side of playing this music. Wynton Marsalis said one time, "A big band score is like a business plan, and if you study it, it will show you the pathway of how to navigate the music and life."

First, if you've made it this far in the book and you struggle with knowing how to read music, then seek out a drum instructor, or even a piano instructor, who can assist you with learning this important skill. I did not learn how to read music until I was about eight years old, and fortunately, my ears grew to hear and navigate music quickly. This sometimes causes me to have to really trust what I am reading versus just listening and trying to figure out the chart. Big band charts can be complex, so it's important to learn how to read. Otherwise, your ears won't always be able to forecast what's coming ahead in the music.

CHAPTER 8: What Is a Big Band Chart?

A big band chart is a diagram and blueprint for an arrangement, but most of what you will play will never be fully represented within the chart.

Navigating a Big Band Chart

The sections that follow outline points and considerations when reading big band charts.

Well-Written vs. Poorly Written Big Band Charts

It's important to understand the difference between well-written and poorly written big band charts. Many composers and arrangers are able to write charts and put the right amount of information in the chart. When that happens, it's great, but you have to know how to read the charts. If it's not a great chart, then you have to learn how to fill in the gaps between what is and isn't on the page. Here's an example of a big band chart for the standard "Cherokee."

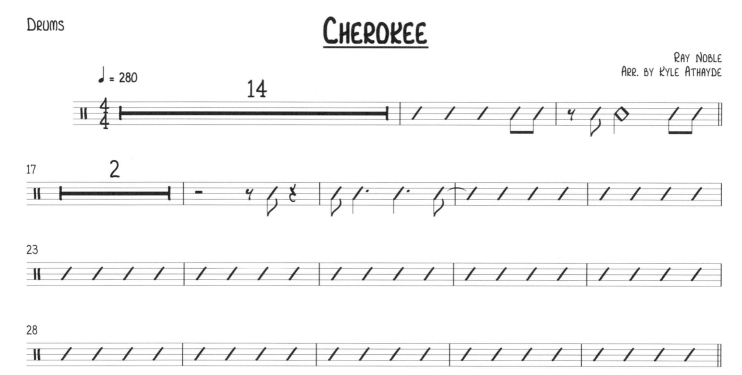

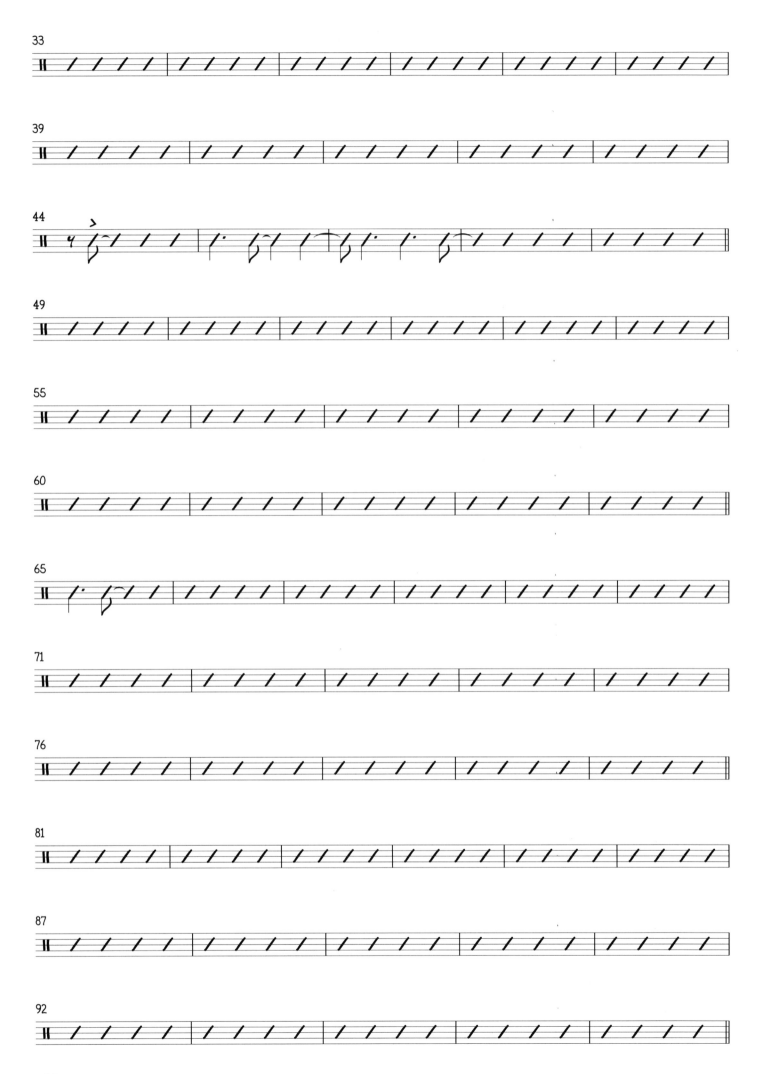

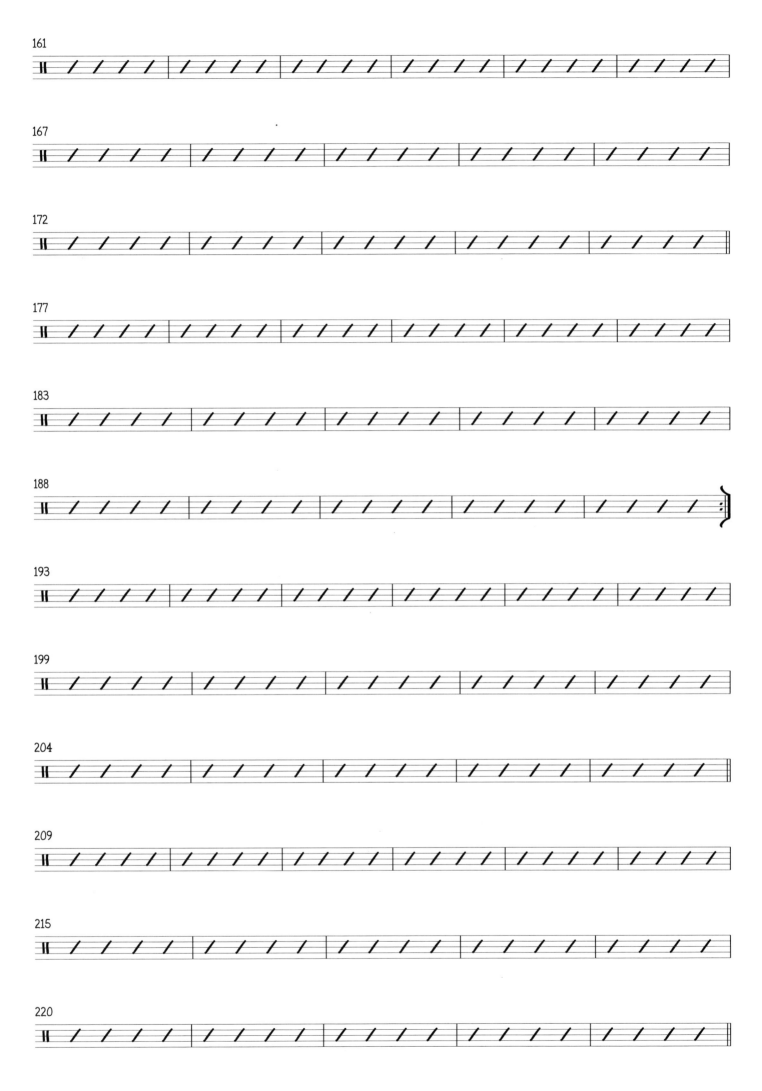

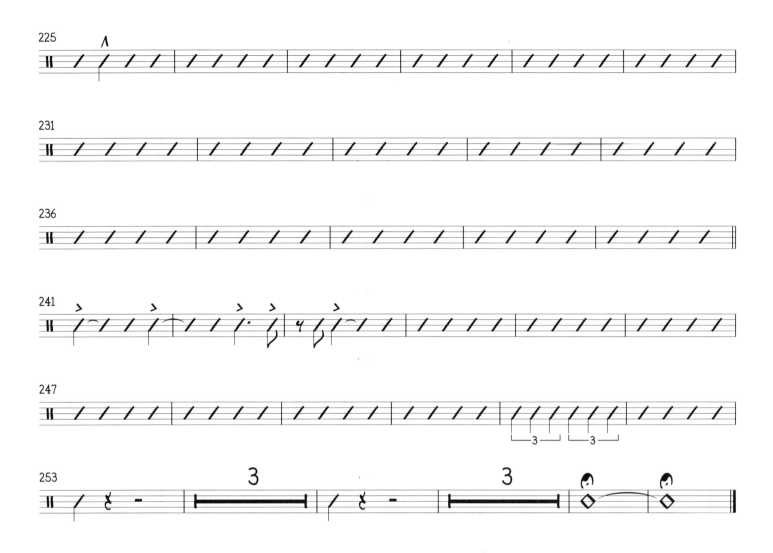

Poorly written charts have either minimal notation or too much notation—making the chart feel over-written. It's important to keep a pen or pencil handy to mark up the parts accordingly.

Making Chart Notes

For the charts that are under-written, you will have to write notes within the chart for yourself. This is important because, unlike in combo playing, you won't remember everything if you don't make notes. Especially, once a big band chart starts, things move really fast.

Playing What's Not Written

I often say most big band charts don't have enough info, or even the right info, for the drummer. So you have to compose your own part on the spot, given what's there in the parts.

Internalizing and Memorizing a Chart

I seek to memorize most charts because I can really take charge of the band when I am not worried about the notes on the page. My first experience with music was via the church, so I feel at my best when I am not reading and playing. This way, I can naturally respond to the music.

Charts with Multiple Pages

Often, when playing big band charts, you will have to navigate multiple pages of music while also trying to play the drum kit simultaneously. Have scotch tape on hand to tape your charts so it's easy to flip and fold them. This will help you avoid interference or stopping the groove. Lastly, make sure your eyes are always looking ahead, which is advice Victor Goines gave me. He taught me that while reading the chart, keep looking ahead so that none of the figures would catch me off guard.

Sight Reading

One of the most important aspects of playing for big band drummers is learning how to sight read, which is the ability to read a chart for the first time with a band. The master big band drummers can do this perfectly.

Sight Reading Tips

- **Initial Scan of the Chart:** When conductors or bandleaders pass out a chart for me, I immediately flip through and try to notice the overall shape of the chart. I try playing through the hits in my head before the director counts off the chart.

- **Don't Get Lost in the Chart:** In the words of Ed Shaughnessy, "This is the cardinal rule for reading any music. It's always important, but even more so in show music, where the drummer most often sets the tempo for each new section. You must constantly be looking ahead for these tempo changes."

- **Keep the Groove Solid:** There have been many times I have read a chart and missed 90% of the hits, but the band didn't realize it because I kept the groove solid. So when in doubt, groove it out!

- **Recognize Repeating Phrases and Hits:** Most big band charts, especially traditional, old-school charts, have very similar forms and hits, so just pay attention and you'll realize you don't have to read a lot of new information.

- **Catch the Big Hits:** Every big band chart has hits that are huge, which are supposed to be caught between the brass and woodwinds. This is what you want to catch. Some of the lighter figures, solis, or backgrounds may not be as big of a deal.

- **Orchestrate on the Fly:** This will be covered more later, but learn how to orchestrate on the kit while sight reading the chart to set up the hits. You never want to sound like you are reading a chart for the first time, even if it is your first time.

- **Pay Attention to Rests:** Rests are within the music for a reason, and ignoring them can show the band that you really are lost.

- **Practice Sight Reading:** The only way you will get better at sight reading a chart is to practice with new charts. Just sharpen your eyes and keep practicing because otherwise, your eyes will get lazy, and over time, your skills may not maintain their strength.

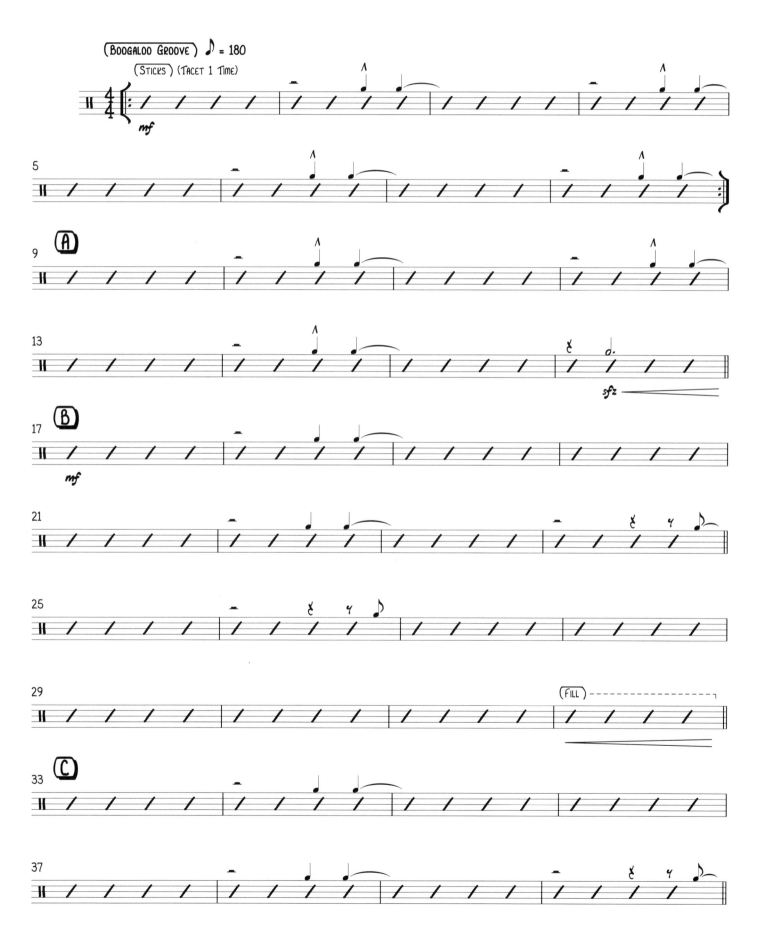

Drums

Soul-Leo

Featuring Russell Malone & The MSU Jazz Ensemble

Mulgrew Miller
Arranged by Jason Hainsworth

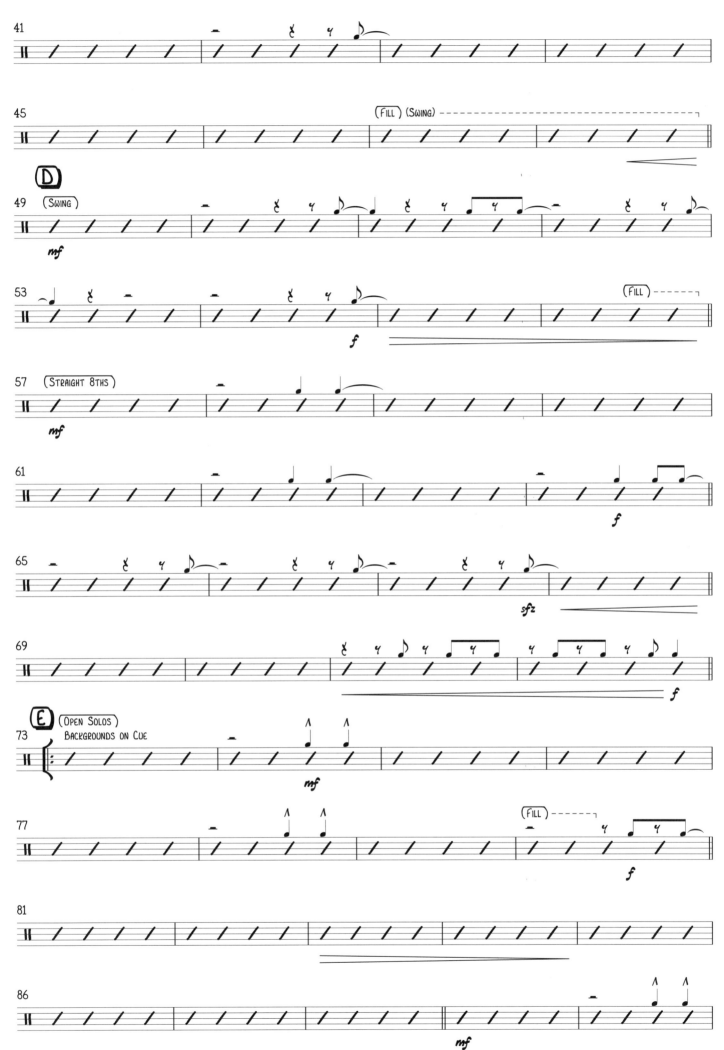

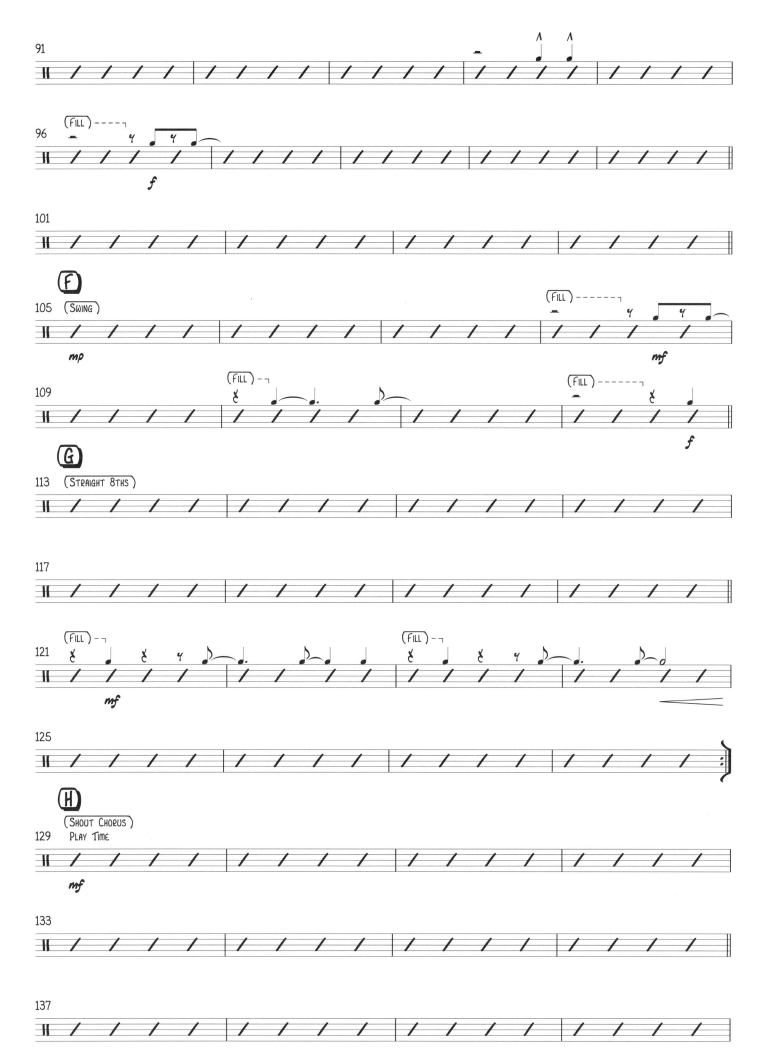

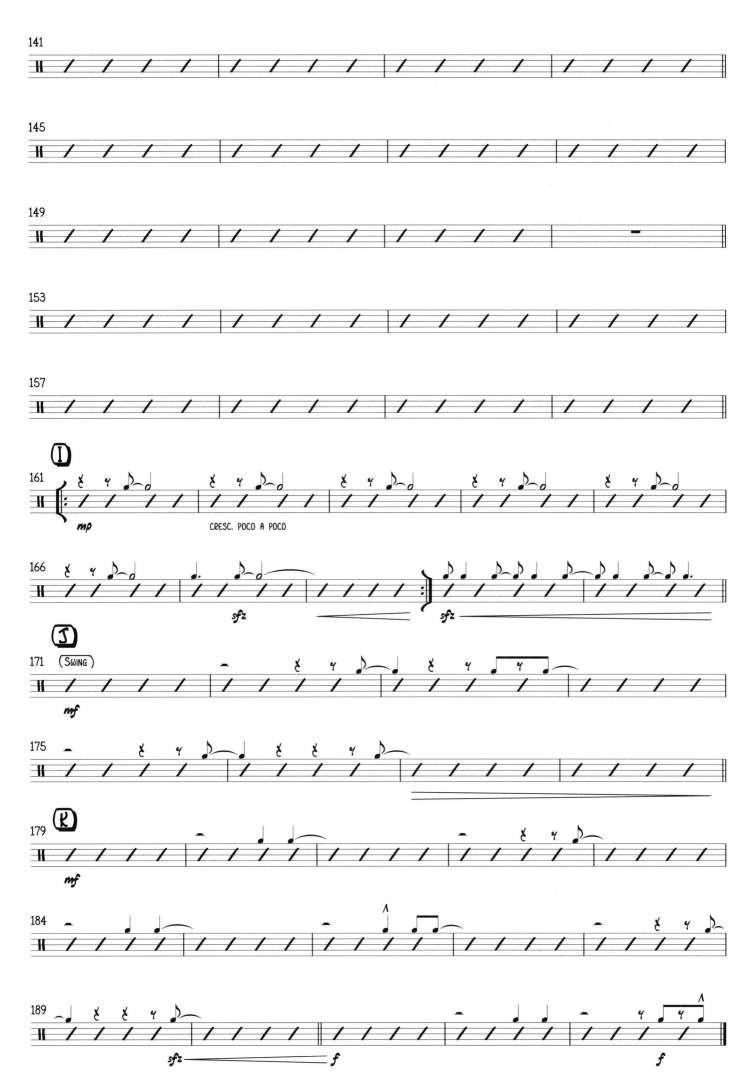

CHAPTER 9: Chart Vocabulary

Before diving into understanding how to play big band charts, here's a crash course in various terms/vocabulary that you will encounter within a chart. One of the books that articulated this concept clearly was written by the great big band legend, Ed Shaughnessy in his book *Show Drumming: The Essential Guide to Playing Drumset for Live Shows and Musicals*, also published by Hal Leonard.

Terms

Tempo

a tempo	return to previous tempo
l'istesso tempo	same tempo
adagio	slow
alla breve	cut time
meno mosso	slower, literally "less motion"
andante	moderately slow
maestoso	slowly, majestically
moderato (mod.)	medium tempo
allegro	fast
accelerando (accel.)	tempo becomes faster
presto	fast, "quickly"
ritardando (rit.)	gradually slower
rallentando (rall.)	gradually slower
rubato	freely
piu mosso	move quickly, literally "more motion"
poco a poco	little by little

Dynamics

pp	extremely soft
p	soft
mp	medium volume, or medium soft
ff	very loud
f	loud
mf	medium loud
cresc.	increasing in volume
fp	loud, then soft, followed by a crescendo
sfz	strong attack and crescendo
dim.	getting softer

Additional Terms

Da Capo (D.C.)	from the top or return to the beginning
Dal Segno (D.S.)	from the sign; return to the sign and repeat the music from there
coda	final section added to the regular form
fermata ⌒	pause or hold; let it ring out
cadenza	improvised passage played freely
cue (on cue)	special entrance dictated by the leader
non troppo	not too much
pesante	heavy
reprise	repeat of music played earlier
segue	move directly to the next section
simile	"almost like" or "similar to" (as on a repeated phrase)
tacit	be silent; no playing
tutti	the full band
solo	featuring one instrument
soli	featuring a section of the orchestra
volti subito (v.s.)	turn the page quickly
double time	tempo moves twice as fast
double time feel	4/4 meter remains, but rhythm section plays twice as fast
cut off //	sudden stop, called "railroad tracks"
"play the ink"	play part exactly as written
eye glasses 6ꝺ	look carefully for an important cue
tag	short extension of the chart
vamp	repeat phrase until the cue to move on
fine	the end

CHAPTER 10: Steps to Big Band Chart Mastery

Three Steps to Learning a Big Band Chart

In my experience, there are three steps to deciphering a big band chart. I apply these steps every time I play a new chart.

1. **Listen to the chart:** Learn to identify the road map of the chart with your ears. Listen to the intro, beginning, solo section, shout section, climax of the chart, and ending. The sooner you're able to hear the patterns in the chart, the sooner you will achieve comfort. This will allow you to support the band and express yourself in the chart.

2. **Play the chart while listening to it:** Many times, some of the fills and markings will look different than how they sound. This makes a big difference in your ability to learn a chart successfully.

3. **Understand that every big band drum chart is incomplete:** There is no perfect big band drum chart because most arrangers and composers simply don't know how to write everything the drummer needs to know within the chart. This is why listening to and playing along with the chart helps. Most of the time, I have to mark up the chart and add additional things that are often missing.

Four Steps to Mastering Playing Jazz Big Band Charts

After learning how to sight read and play through a big band chart, you can move on to mastering these charts, done in four steps:

1. **Overall/Objective Chart Study:** This kind of listening is equivalent to seeing a painting for the first time and viewing it from far back with no intensive study, but just taking it in. I typically listen to a chart three to four times just to understand the sound of the band and the arrangement.

2. **Roadmap Study:** This is when I listen but with my chart on the iPad; I also use an Apple Pencil or the Marker within the Apple Books app. At this point, I am listening while looking at the chart, and I make sure the form lines up with what I see on the chart.

3. **Study Drum Chart Vocabulary:** Next, it's important for me to study the drummer's approach on the album, especially if it's one of the masters like Papa Jo, Sonny Payne, Sonny Greer, Mel Lewis, or a host of other drum masters. With this perspective, I am going to seek to copy their approach but with my own sound and adjustments. If it's a younger drummer, then I'll check out what they are doing if it's working for the chart. If what they are doing doesn't work, I'll immediately seek to find some different musical solutions. I listen to how they orchestrate and phrase everything.

4. **Study the Drummer Who Performed the Chart:** It's important to make sure you study the masters of this music, and that's probably the most redundant statement you will read throughout this book. You will not master any form of music without listening to it. Regarding big band drumming, checking out how the drummer supports the band always gives you a great starting point.

CHAPTER 11: Listening to the Band While Reading the Chart

Listening 101 in a Big Band

One of the most important keys to improving your big band drumming is through listening. Most of what makes the big band difficult are the challenges one may have with listening. The difference between hearing and listening is crucial.

- **Listening:** The ability to actively observe what is going on every second within the chart, being aware of each motif and phrase.

- **Hearing:** The overall observation of a piece or chart in its entirety with no further exploration of the role you play within the music; you are merely appreciating the piece.

Listening Priorities

When listening to the big band, it is tempting to listen to everything at once, but your ears have to compartmentalize sections and listen in stages and levels. Otherwise, it will be overwhelming to take it all in.

Hearing over the Band

The insight from master drummers goes a long way in the journey to master big band drumming. Herlin Riley is one of my favorite big band drummers. He embodies the confidence and tradition and truly understands the art form of big band drumming. Herlin gave me some great advice years ago when he was in the Lincoln Center Jazz Orchestra led by Wynton Marsalis. He said to me, "Ulysses, you have to physically exist behind the kit playing drums while your ears are out in front of the band."

I apply that advice to combo drumming as well, but it's very applicable to big band drumming because it allows you to have a full-scale perspective of listening, which is key to this style of drumming. You will never master a chart and balance with the big band if you don't have an objective approach to listening while playing in the large ensemble context.

Avoiding Distractions

Remember: Don't overplay. Playing time is the most important thing. Many times within the big band, we become distracted by our own playing, listening to ourselves and not the band.

Listening to the Bassist

In a big band, think of yourself as the anchor that is holding the band down. You are at the bottom of the ocean, keeping everything together. The connection to the chain is what keeps the anchor connected to the vessel. The drums are the anchor, the bass is the chain, and together, you work collectively to keep the band together and solid. You must learn to listen to the bassist as part of playing successfully with the bassist. Walking bass lines and the pulse of the rhythm are focal points that one should listen to while playing. Make sure you are in the right proximity to the bass player, and consider that they may need an amp or microphone. If you can set up close to them, you probably won't need the amp.

Listening to the Pianist

The comping rhythms from the pianist are important for the drummer and the rest of the rhythm section to lock in with. There are multiple connective points for the pianist, bassist, and drummer.

Listening to the Rhythm Section

The rhythm section must listen to each other and play together. However, you must first be able to identify each instrument individually and then ascertain how to listen to them collectively.

Listening to the Lead Trumpeter

After anchoring yourself within the rhythm section, the next important voice in the band for the drummer is the lead trumpeter. Many of the major hits in the chart will be initiated by the high voice in the band, which is lead trumpet. Also, they are the unofficial leader of the horn section, and the lead alto sax and lead trombone take their cues from the lead trumpeter. You don't want to be disconnected from or tick off the lead trumpeter—work in tandem with them. Often, when the chart doesn't contain the right information, I consult with the lead trumpeter and check out their part.

Listening to the Brass

The trumpets and trombones are the power within the big band, and the "big" sound comes from their parts. Ninety percent of what is written in most charts is coming from the brass section. I was very intimidated for many years by the brass, but when I became more confident, they weren't a threat to me and we began to work together, musically.

Listening to the Saxophone Section

The melody and counter line of the band comes from the sweet and sultry saxophone section. Often, if drummers aren't cautious and aware of overplaying, they can overpower the saxophones.

Listening to the Conductor

Most high school and college bands have a conductor, but the drummer is the unofficial conductor in the band. You must strike a healthy balance between listening to the band and honoring the choices of the conductor. You'll be able to strike the perfect balance over time.

Listening Test

In this section, I want you to test your ears on listening. Choose one song for this test because it's more about your ears, not the composition. A good tune to start with is the Count Basie recording of "Splanky" from the *Live at the Sands* album. For listening sources, use headphones, external speakers, Bluetooth speakers, or car speakers.

- **Listen to the Entire Big Band:** Check out the sound of the tune and get the overall perspective on the sound of the band.

- **Listen to the Rhythm Section:** Check out the relationship between the pianist, bassist, guitarist, and drummer. Don't pay attention to the horns quite yet.

- **Listen to the Trumpet Section:** Check out each trumpet and discern between the parts.

- **Listen to the Trombone Section:** Decipher the different parts within the trombone section and their roles within the music.

- **Listen to the Saxophone Section:** Check out the difference between the alto, tenor, and baritone saxophones and understand their role within the music.

- **Avoiding Distractions:** The most challenging thing about listening to music—especially nowadays—is the focus issue; make sure that you eliminate distractions while listening. If you are unable to focus while listening, you'll miss the magic in this assignment.

CHAPTER 12: Arranging and Orchestration 101

As a drummer, you spend most of your formal education learning how to play grooves and understand the timing of a song. But, you don't really approach the topic of arranging and orchestration. Most popular music (funk, rock, metal, gospel, etc.) doesn't directly approach the idea of arranging and orchestration from the drummer's perspective.

Defining Arranging and Orchestration

What Is Arranging?

Essentially, arranging is organizing a group of ideas into a piece of music or a chart. Regarding jazz, arranging involves a musical form (AABA, ABAC, 12-bar blues, etc.) with a statement of the melody, other sections, and various re-statements of melodies. Often, in big band music, you will also see a shout section, solis, and solo sections with extended forms. It's important as a drummer to understand the various forms that are present in the music; this will help us understand how to play our role effectively.

What Is Orchestration?

Orchestration is how we respond to arranged ideas, and the great drummers of the big band era understood that completely. For example, when a hit is played on beat 4, often times, you will hear a jazz drummer play the bass drum and a crash cymbal to accent it. This creates a big moment in the chart that elevates it, versus not playing or accenting the beat at all.

When studying arranging and orchestration, there are four entry points to understanding it.

1. First, listen to a record.

2. Listen to how the drummer plays time throughout the piece.

3. Listen to the hits the drummer plays and compare them to the hits that are marked in the chart.

4. Listen to the parts of the drumset that the drummer plays to accentuate the hits within the chart.

After studying a record or live performance with this perspective, you will begin the journey of orchestrating and arranging on the kit. You can also speak to the arranger or the conductor of the band about what they prefer as well. I played a gig recently with John Clayton, and he was very specific about how he wanted certain things orchestrated on the kit, even parts of how I soloed. As a brilliant arranger, he hears everything in context and has a framework for how it's all supposed to fit together.

Melody, Harmony, and Variation

In order to be effective in your orchestration on the drum kit, it's important to know the definitions of melody, harmony, and variation.

- Melody is a single-note line or idea that is the focal point of the song.

- Harmony is the chordal language to support the melodic idea.

- Variation is the re-arranging and re-capitulation of these ideas throughout the song.

Hearing the Melody

It's important as a drummer to recognize the melody immediately and allow that to inform what you play and how you support the band.

Catching the Hits

There is a terminology used in the big band world when the band or conductor will tell you to "catch the hits." This means you must study the hits that are marked in the chart. You must also remember to listen for what isn't notated. "Catching the hits" simply means musically acknowledging all of the information that is in the chart, and orchestration is crucial to how you catch the hits. Here are some tips:

- Hits involving trumpets: Use the snare drum and crash cymbal.

- Hits involving brass section: Use the cymbals and bass drum.

- Hits involving trombones: Use the low end of the kit.

- There is also the Mel Lewis school of catching hits, which involves playing time continuously while also catching the hits.

Orchestration takes years to understand fully. Studying the master big band drummers gives you a clue into understanding what are either standard or unique ways to orchestrate the big band chart that you are currently working on.

Solis

Most arrangers will compose a soli, or a passage that highlights a lot of collective rhythmic and melodic phrasing within a section. It often focuses on the instrumental section that is being featured, such as the saxophone section.

Shout Sections

The big climax section before the re-statement of the melody is often the shout section, and it's probably the most important section for a drummer in the chart. If you mess up the shout section, then you are most likely getting fired. It's our moment to shine, so that's why internalizing it is very helpful.

Vocal Charts

Most current big bands often include a vocalist, which can present a unique art form when playing hits. You have to support a big band while also not getting in the way of the vocalist. Many of the great big band drummers have accomplished this. Here are a few things to consider:

- Outline the time.

- Maintain a present but sensitive volume.

- Learn the vocal lyric.

- If a backbeat or shuffle is required, don't hold back.

- Create dynamic levels when the vocalist is singing and also when the band is being featured within the arrangement.

Part 5: Learning from the Masters

Jazz drumming was founded by great musicians who helped create this art from the beginning in the late 1800s. Big band drumming started between 1915–1920, and it was fully established in the 1920s. Some of the greatest big band records were made from 1920 to 1990. Study them fully because the key to everything that you want to add to your playing is within the recordings that have been left for us. In my own case, I became a better big band drummer by listening to records and playing with them.

CHAPTER 13: Confidence with the Big Band

I remember when I first heard the big band next to me in high school. To be honest, I was a bit intimidated because it was a lot of sound coming from these musicians, and I didn't quite know what to do. When you play with a smaller configuration of musicians, it's easier to have confidence because you are responsible for fewer people. However, the first thing you must access as a drummer is tapping fully into your new level of confidence. Without it, you will not be an adequate drummer and certainly not what the band needs.

Ways to Work on Your Confidence

Many of the challenges I hear with young big band drummers involve their lack of confidence. Here are a few ways to work on your confidence and feel solid about some important things.

Your Playing

If you are insecure about your playing, then that will carry over to the band. So you must practice and gain experience playing in real time to solidify your confidence in yourself and your musicianship. Steve Turre told me years ago, "You practice to alleviate the instrument as an obstacle in expressing yourself."

Your Ability to Read and Understand the Chart

Growing up in church, I always struggled with reading because my ears could hear something much faster than I could read it. So big band used to be really hard for me because I would barely read, and instead, I would rely on my ears. I have had to do a great deal of work on really paying attention to the chart and making sure that I am not relying solely on my ears.

Knowledge That You Are the Unofficial Conductor

Many of the musicians in a big band think that they are the most important person on the bandstand. The truth is that they are indeed important, but the most important person in the music and on the bandstand is the drummer. Not to be arrogant, but the drummer has the power to make or break the band. I always say that we are the most powerful member of the band, but we must use our powers for good and not for evil. When you fully understand the magnitude of that power, then it's easy to fully accept it and utilize it with wisdom.

Don't Broadcast Your Mistakes

Most of the audience members are unaware of the details of the chart. So when they see it on your face that you missed something or messed up, it's because you've allowed your emotions to get involved and tell on yourself.

Deal with Your Musical Insecurities

Here's a true story that happened to me recently… I was scheduled to play with the incredible John Clayton at the Cleveland Tri-C Jazz Fest, filling in for the great drummer, Jeff Hamilton.

The charts were challenging, but more importantly, I was very insecure about the music and filling in for Jeff, who is one of the best big band drummers alive. So, during the rehearsal, I have to be honest: I completely bombed. I could see the look on John's face, like, "What's going on with this guy?" (At least, that was my perception.) I was messing up on stuff that, in the back of my mind, I knew I could do, but more importantly, I had let the energy of the moment get into my psyche. A lot of reasons could have been the source of my nervousness, like the fact I hadn't been playing as many gigs recently, etc. However, for all of us, it's always something that can get into our head, and until we deal with it, we won't overcome it. I was basically sabotaging the moment musically with my nervous energy.

After soundcheck, I went back to my room, meditated, and prayed; I literally looked in the mirror and said, "Dude, get over yourself; you got this, and you can play this music in your sleep." I actually believed it and accepted it. I went back that night, and the gig was amazing. John texted me the next morning, telling me how much he loved my approach to the music. Moral of the story: Have confidence in yourself, no matter what!

CHAPTER 14: Big Band Playlist

The drummers listed below have been impactful to my playing and understanding of the art of big band drumming. It's important to know that this list reflects those who I feel are important to mention in the canon of big band drumming, many of who are often forgotten within previously published books.

In my humble opinion, many of these giants never received the level of acknowledgment and appreciation that is well-deserved for their efforts. Here are their names and recordings so that their lives are acknowledged and their contributions are fully recognized. There are many recordings out there, but I chose to list at least one for each drummer, so make sure you do your research and check out everyone's discography!

1900s–1970s

Artie Shaw
Buddy Rich, "Traffic Jam"
Cliff Leeman, "Born to Swing"

Billy Eckstine
Art Blakey, *Jazz Manifesto: Art Blakey*

Buddy Rich Band
Buddy Rich, "Mercy, Mercy, Mercy"

Count Basie Orchestra
Butch Miles, *Basie Big Band*
David Gibson, *Live at El Morocco*
   (Directed by Frank Foster)
Dennis Mackrel, "88 Basie Street"
Harold Jones, "Ain't Misbehavin'"
Papa Jo Jones, *The Old Count and the
   New Count*
Sonny Payne, *April in Paris*

Chick Webb Band
Chick Webb, *Chick Webb
   and His Orchestra*

Dizzy Gillespie
Charlie Persip, *Dizzy Gillespie at Newport*

Duke Ellington
Louis Bellson, *Ellington Uptown*
Rufus Speedy Jones, *The Far East Suite*
Sam Woodyard, *Such Sweet Thunder,
   The Nutcracker Suite*

Frank Sinatra
Irving Cottler, "Love Is Here to Stay"

Gene Krupa Band
Gene Krupa, "Sing, Sing, Sing"

Glenn Miller Orchestra
Ray McKinley, *The New Glenn Miller
   Orchestra*
Maurice Purtill, *Glenn Miller and
   His Orchestra*

Gerry Mulligan Band
Mel Lewis, *Gerry Mulligan and the
   Concert Jazz Band at the Village Vanguard*

Harry James Orchestra
Louis Bellson, *Harry James and
   His Orchestra*

Jimmie Lunceford
Jimmy Crawford,
   Jimmie Lunceford and His Orchestra

Louis Armstrong Band
Sid Catlett, "Please Stop
   Playing Those Blues Boy"

Oliver Nelson
Ed Shaughnessy, *Full Nelson*
   (Tracks 1, 2, 8, 9)
Osie Johnson, *Full Nelson*
   (All Other Tracks)

Quincy Jones
Grady Tate, "Walking in Space"

Stan Kenton Band
Shelly Manne, *The Kenton Era*
Stan Levey, *Sketches on Standards*

Thelonious Monk Orchestra
Art Taylor, *At Town Hall*

Tommy Dorsey Band
Buddy Rich, "Well, Git It," "Yes Indeed"
Dave Tough, *Tribute to Dorsey, Volume 1*

Woody Herman
Dave Tough, "Apple Honey"
Gene Krupa, *Best of the Big Bands Vol. 7*
Jake Hanna, *The Swingin'est Big Band Ever*

1980s–Present

**Arturo O'Farrill and the
Afro Latin Jazz Orchestra**
Vince Cherico, "The Offense of the Drum"

Bob Brookmeyer
Charlie Persip, *Jazz Is a Kick*

Christian McBride Big Band
Quincy Phillips, *For Jimmy,
    Wes and Oliver*
Ulysses Owens Jr., *The Good Feeling*

**Clayton-Hamilton
Jazz Orchestra**
Jeff Hamilton, *Live at MCG*

**Frank Foster and the
Loud Minority**
Charlie Persip, *Shiny Stockings*

Generation Gap Jazz Orchestra
Ulysses Owens Jr., *Generation Gap
    Jazz Orchestra*

Gil Evans Orchestra
Charlie Persip, *Out of the Cool*

GRP All-Star Big Band
Dave Weckl, *GRP All-Star Big Band*

Gordon Goodwin Big Phat Band
Bernie Dresel, *Swingin' for the Fences*

Joe Henderson
Al Foster, *Big Band*
Joe Chambers, *Big Band*
Lewis Nash, *Big Band*
Paulinho Braga, *Big Band*

John Beasley's Monk'Estra
Terreon Gully, *Monk'estra
    Plays John Beasley*
Vinnie Colaiuta, *Monk'estra
    Plays John Beasley*
Ulysses Owens Jr., *Monk'estra Plays
    John Beasley*

John Hollenbeck
John Hollenbeck, *Songs I Like a Lot*

Maria Schneider Orchestra
Clarence Penn, *Concert in the Garden*
Johnathan Blake, *Data Lords*

Maynard Ferguson
Frankie Dunlop, *A Message from Birdland*
Gregg Bissonette, *Live from San Francisco*
Peter Erskine, *Carnival*
Dave Tull, *Big Bop Nouveau*
Stu Martin, *Newport Suite*

Miho Hazama Orchestra
Jake Goldbas, *Dancer in Nowhere*

Revive Big Band
John Davis, (Upcoming Release)

Steven Feifke Big Band
Bryan Carter, *Kinetic*
Jimmy Macbride, *Kinetic*
Ulysses Owens Jr., *Kinetic*

Thad Jones/Mel Lewis Orchestra
Mel Lewis, *Live at the Village Vanguard*
    and *Presenting Joe Williams and
    Thad Jones/Mel Lewis, the Jazz Orchestra*

Ulysses Owens Jr. Big Band
Ulysses Owens Jr., *Soul Conversations*

Vanguard Jazz Orchestra
John Riley, *Can I Persuade You?*

Wynton Marsalis, Jazz at Lincoln Center Orchestra
Ali Jackson, *Portrait in Seven Shades* and *The Music of Wayne Shorter*
Herlin Riley, *Big Train, A Love Supreme, Blood on the Fields*
Jason Marsalis, *All Rise*
Obed Calvaire, *The Democracy Suite*

Some of My Favorite Big Band Drummers

Here are some drummers whose approach to big band drumming I just love. I have experienced their artistry live, but can't point to a specific recording of their playing; however, they are worth checking out!

Charles Goold

Evan Sherman

Kenny Washington

Lewis Nash

Tommy Igoe

CHAPTER 15: Big Band Charts

It's important for me to have charts within the book for you to study and check out my approach with my big band, playing some of my favorite arrangements. I hope you enjoy them!

"London Towne" (Poinciana Groove)

Composer: Benny Benack III

Arranger: Steven Feifke

Reference Recordings

Ulysses Owens Jr. Big Band, *Soul Conversations*

Ahmad Jamal, *At the Pershing: But Not for Me*, "Poinciana"

Performance Notes

The groove is crucial to making this song feel great. This is because it's a long form, and the chart builds slowly over the course of the five to six minutes of playing it. The foundation of this groove derives from the great drummer Vernel Fournier, who was an incredible groove master and brush player from New Orleans. (I have often said there is something really special about New Orleans drummers.) This groove focuses on the ride cymbal playing on beats 2 and 4. The bass drum is utilized as an anticipator to move the groove, emphasizing the prominent bass line.

Before taking on the chart, the first thing I would do is spend time playing the groove. Once you feel comfortable with it, focus on catching the hits while still keeping the groove solid.

Drums

London Towne

Composed by Benny Benack III
Arranged by Steven Feifke

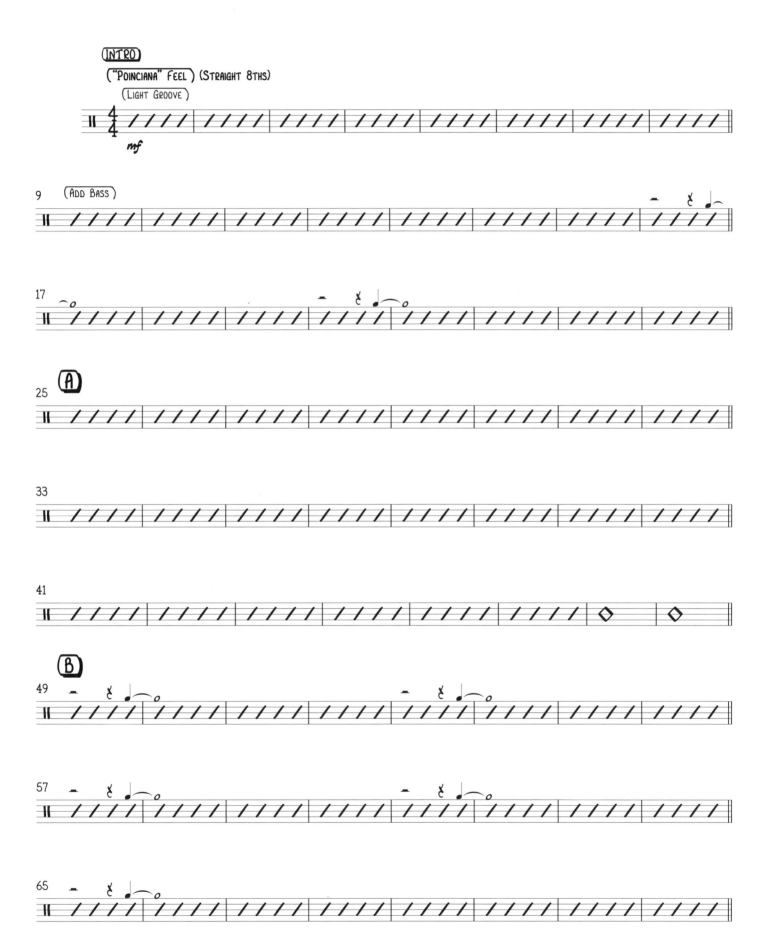

60

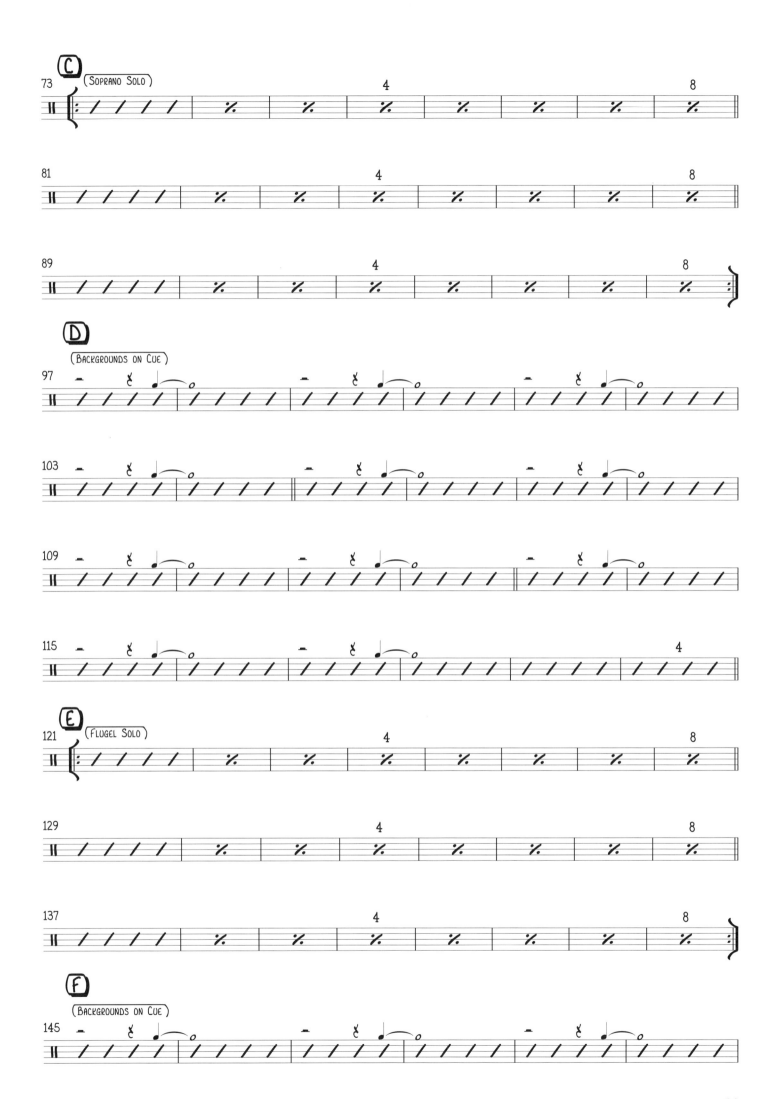

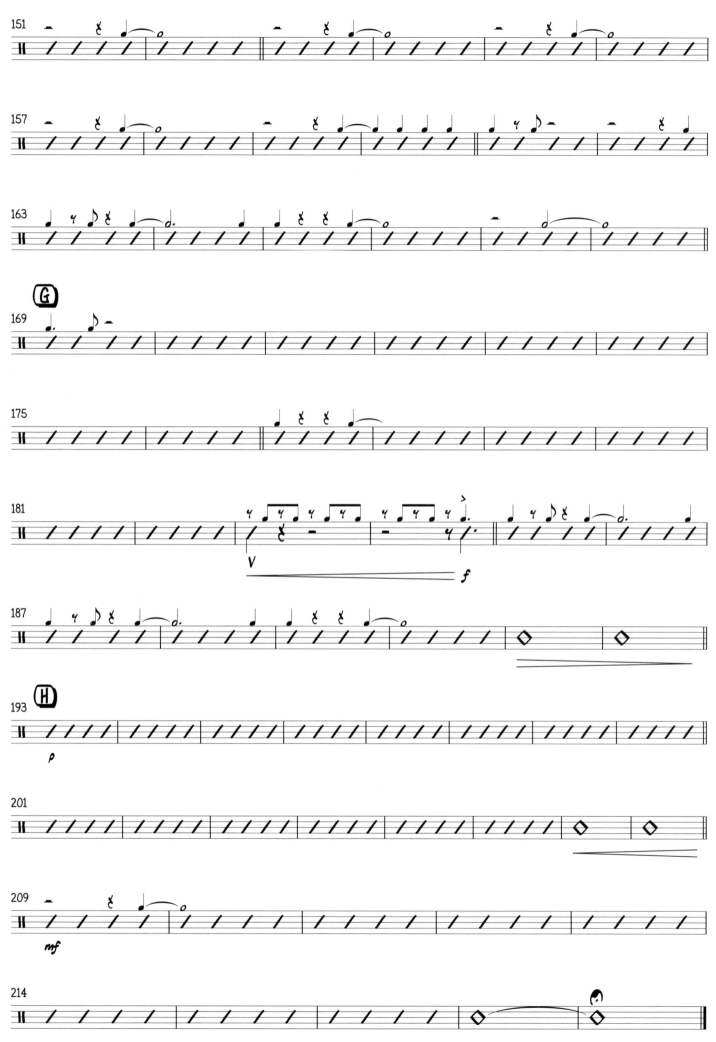

"Two Bass Hit" (Uptempo Swing)

Composer: Dizzy Gillespie, John Lewis

Arranger: Michael Dease

Reference Recordings

Ulysses Owens Jr. Big Band, *Soul Conversations*

Michael Dease, *Relentless*

Performance Notes

The key to performing uptempo swing is your technique and being able to keep the groove solid so that the band doesn't fall apart. Playing uptempo has to be worked out in the shed so that when you play with the band, you are confident about what you are able to accomplish. Focus on playing the ride cymbal, then play strongly on beats 2 and 4 with your foot on the hi-hat with some light feathering on the bass drum. There will be moments when you will want to implement a rimshot on beat 4.

Drums

Two Bass Hit

Music by Dizzy Gillespie and John Lewis
Arranged by Michael Dease

"Girl Talk" (Walking Ballad)

Composer: Neal Hefti

Arranger: Yasushi Nakamura

Reference Recordings

Ulysses Owens Jr. Big Band, *Soul Conversations*

Count Basie with the Alan Copeland Singers, *Basie Swingin' Voices Singin'*

Performance Notes

"Girl Talk" is a sexy walking ballad, which means that you have to focus on the pulse of the tune, understanding that less is more. For the first part of the tune, I recommend using brushes with beats 2 and 4 played on the hi-hat with your foot. As the tune builds, switch to sticks and play a little bit heavier. Once the bigger figures start appearing in the tune, bring the band up in energy and shape the parts. Then, bring the band back down to address the beginning groove. This is a very mature chart, and it takes studying the tune and listening to all the ensemble parts to give the band what they need.

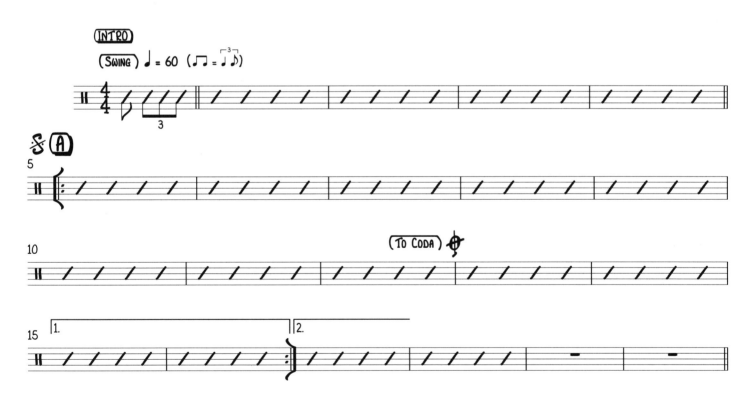

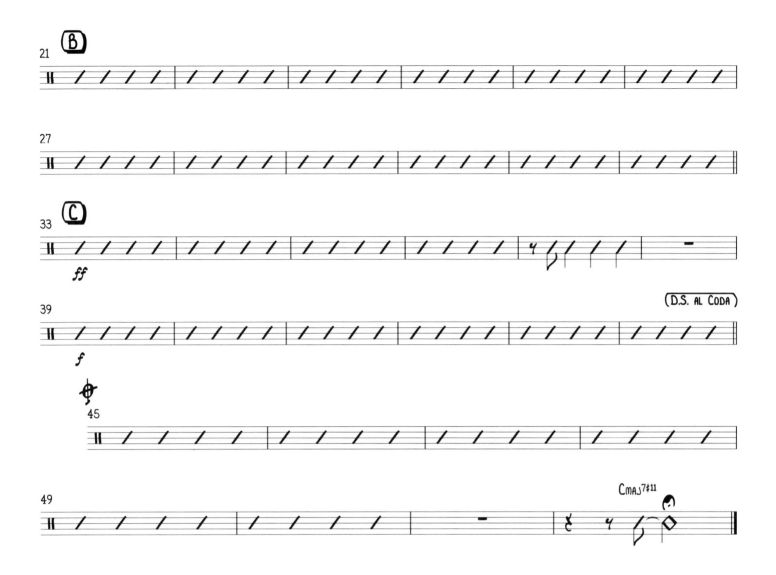

"Giant Steps" (Medium Swing)

Composer: John Coltrane

Arranger: Diego Rivera

Reference Recordings

Ulysses Owens Jr. Big Band, *Soul Conversations*

John Coltrane, *Giant Steps*

Performance Notes

The key to this chart is playing uptempo with energy yet not over-playing. You have to really pace yourself and make sure that it's not just a busy swing feel. Make sure each fill and punctuation makes sense within the intricate figures of the chart.

Giant Steps

Music by John Coltrane
Arranged by Diego Rivera

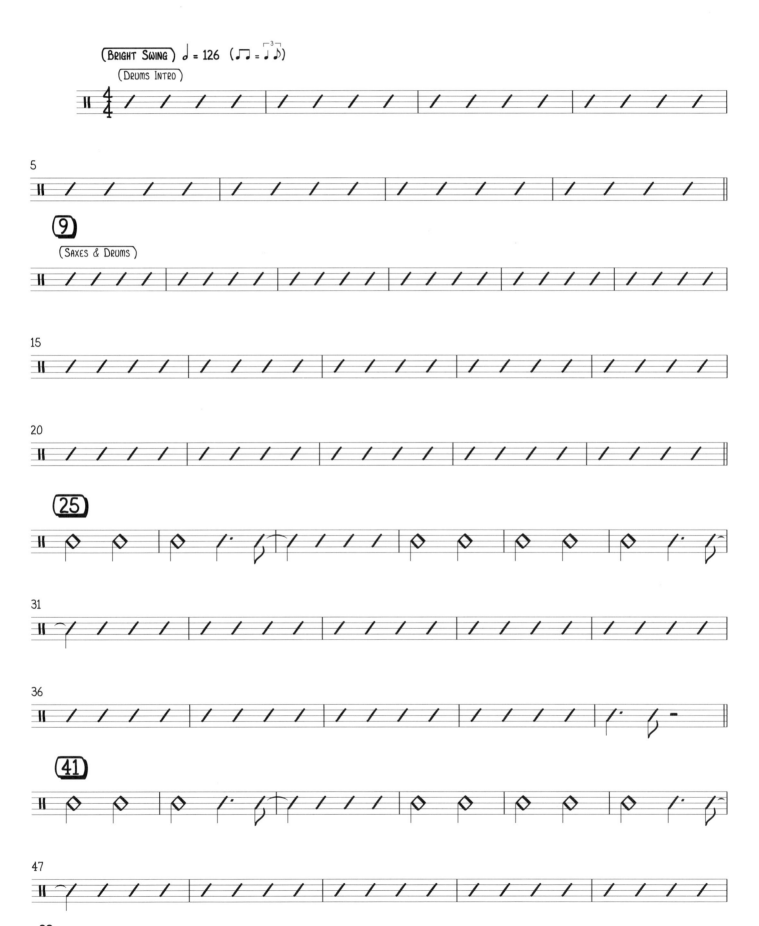

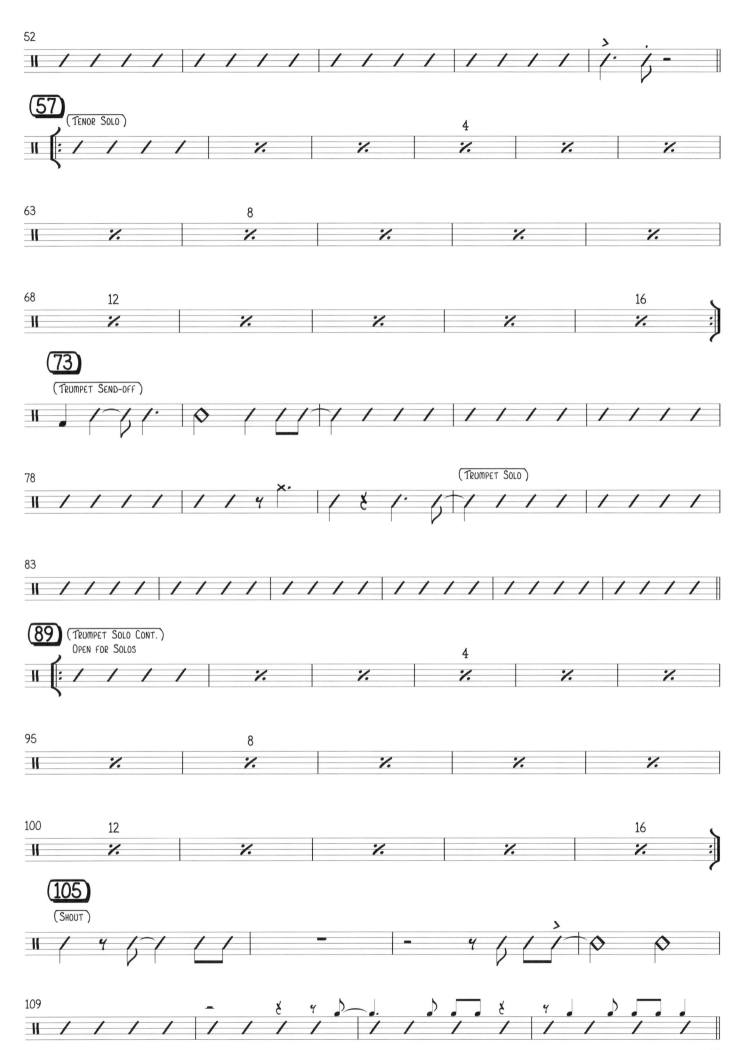

"Language of Flowers" (Slow Ballad)

Composer: Yasushi Nakamura

Arranger: Yasushi Nakamura

Reference Recordings

Ulysses Owens Jr. Big Band, *Soul Conversations*

Yasushi Nakamura, *A Lifetime Treasure*

New Century Jazz Quintet, *Time Is Now*

Performance Notes

Traditional ballad playing with brushes is key here, making sure that your sweeping patterns are strong on beats 1, 2, 3, and 4. Once the band opens up, I shift to playing with sticks for a short moment; however, I mainly focus on brush playing with a strong time to support the alto saxophonist.

Language of Flowers

Composed and Arranged by Yasushi Nakamura

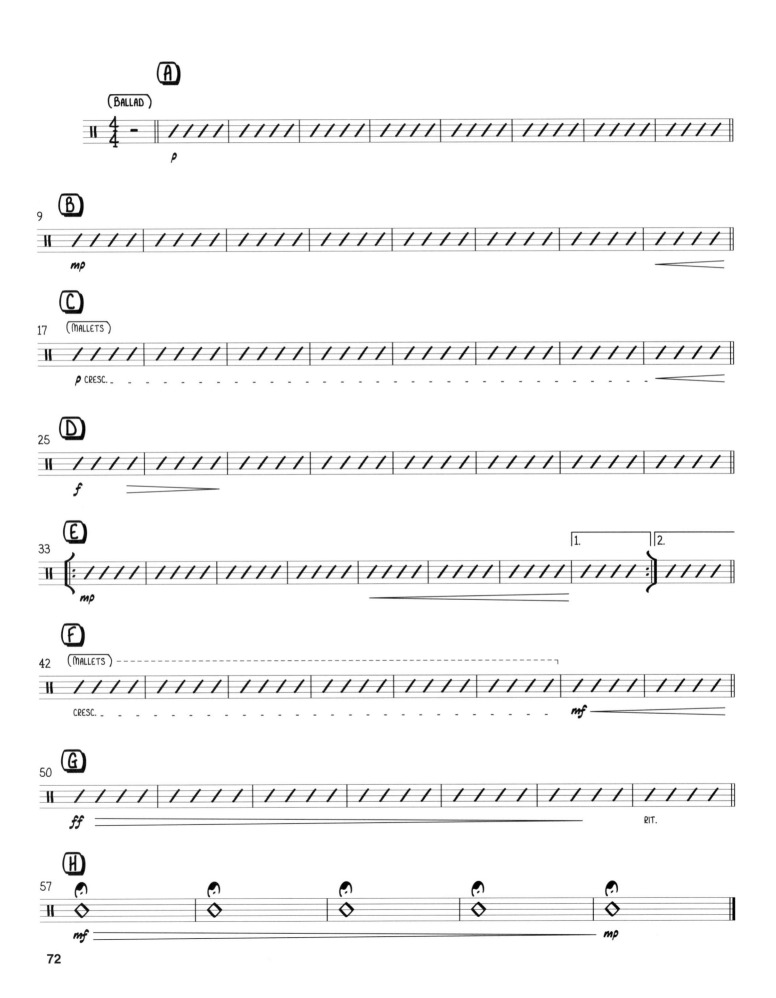

"Red Chair" (Waltz/Modern)

Composer: Ulysses Owens Jr.

Arranger: Michael Thomas

Reference Recordings

Ulysses Owens Jr. Big Band, *Soul Conversations*

U.O. Project, *It's Time for U*

Performance Notes

Waltz drum playing is tricky because it relies on making sure every facet of the tune has the support of the drums. This tune has a lot of transitions within it. It starts with basic 3/4 brush patterns; then, once the solos begin, I switch to sticks. Once the trombone soli happens, it's time to give strong but light time to support the trombones and prepare for the counterpoint section that happens later in the tune. The key to this composition is really understanding how to support the band through various transitions while still conveying time.

Drums

Red Chair

Composed by Ulysses Owens Jr.
Arranged by Michael Thomas

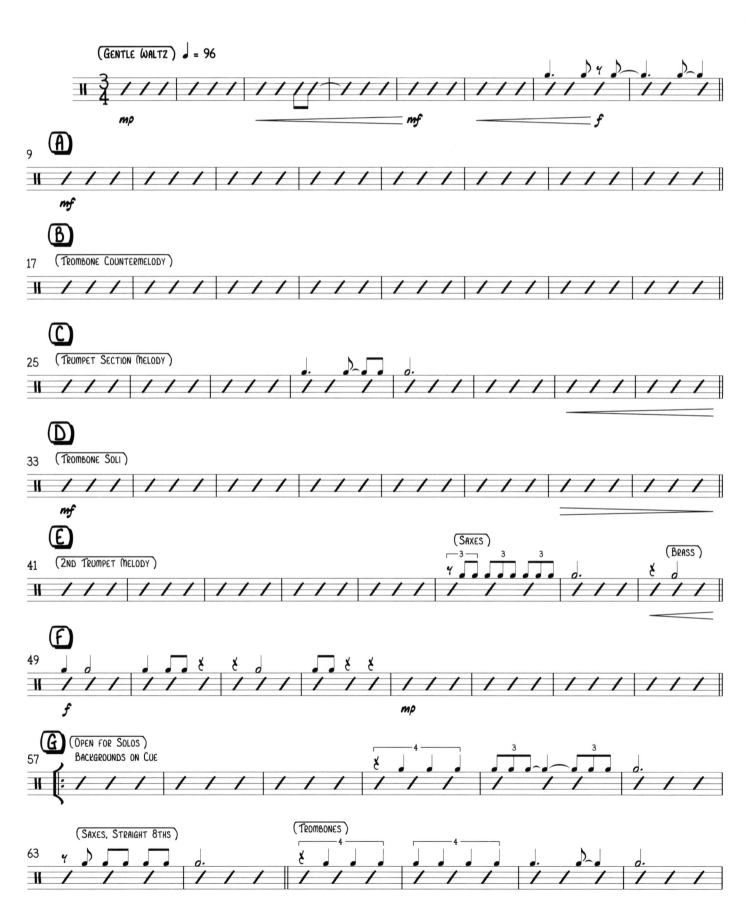

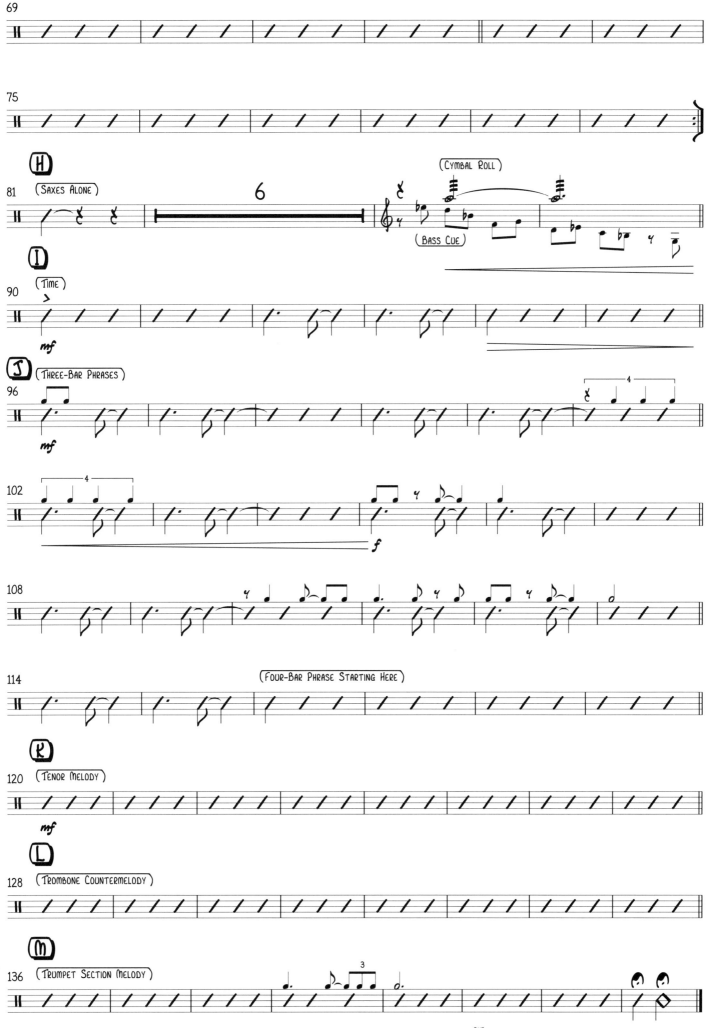

"Human Nature" (Funk)

Composers: Steve Porcaro, John Bettis

Arranger: Michael Thomas

Reference Recordings

Ulysses Owens Jr. Big Band, *Soul Conversations*

Michael Jackson, *Thriller*

Performance Notes

One of my favorite compositions in music is "Human Nature," and this chart possesses a lot of the key elements that drew me to this tune. However, it's important to not overplay on groove tunes with a big band; instead, you must dynamically follow the arc of the tune.

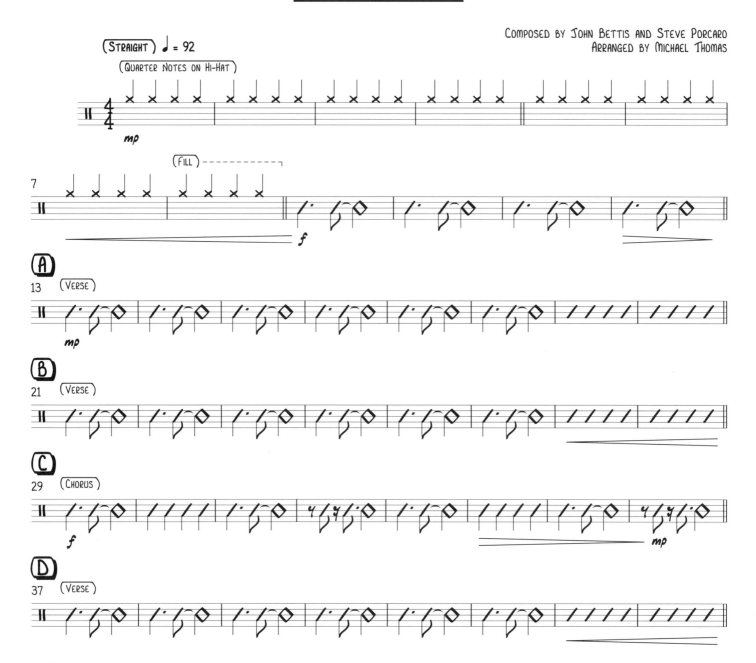

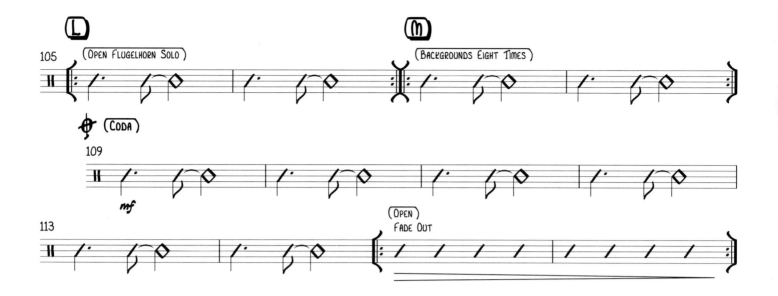

"Beardom X" (Swing)

Composer: Ulysses Owens Jr., Mike Cottone

Arranger: Diego Rivera

Reference Recordings

Ulysses Owens Jr. Big Band, *Soul Conversations*

Ulysses Owens Jr., *Unanimous*

Performance Notes

Elvin Jones! He is the inspiration for my approach to this tune with a relaxed, open swing feel that leaves space.

Drums

BEARDOM X

MUSIC BY ULYSSES OWENS JR. AND MIKE COTTONE
ARRANGED BY DIEGO RIVERA

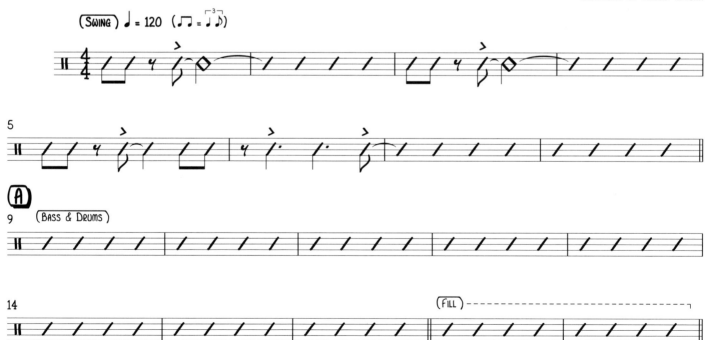

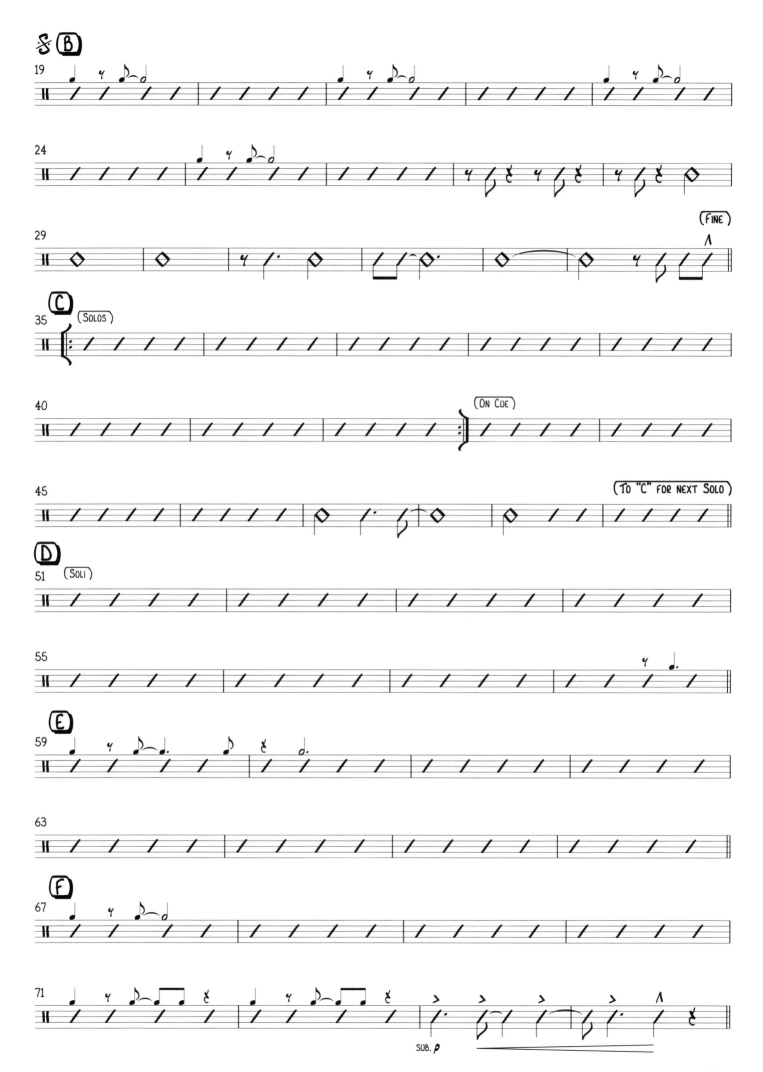

"Harlem Harlem Harlem" (Shuffle)

Composer: Charles Turner III

Arranger: Steven Feifke

Reference Recordings

Ulysses Owens Jr. Big Band, *Soul Conversations*

Charles Turner & Uptown Swing, "Harlem Harlem Harlem"

Performance Notes

The Art Blakey shuffle is the key here. Allow the power of the shuffle to drive and carry the band.

Drums

Harlem Harlem Harlem

Composed by Charles Turner
Arranged by Steven Feifke

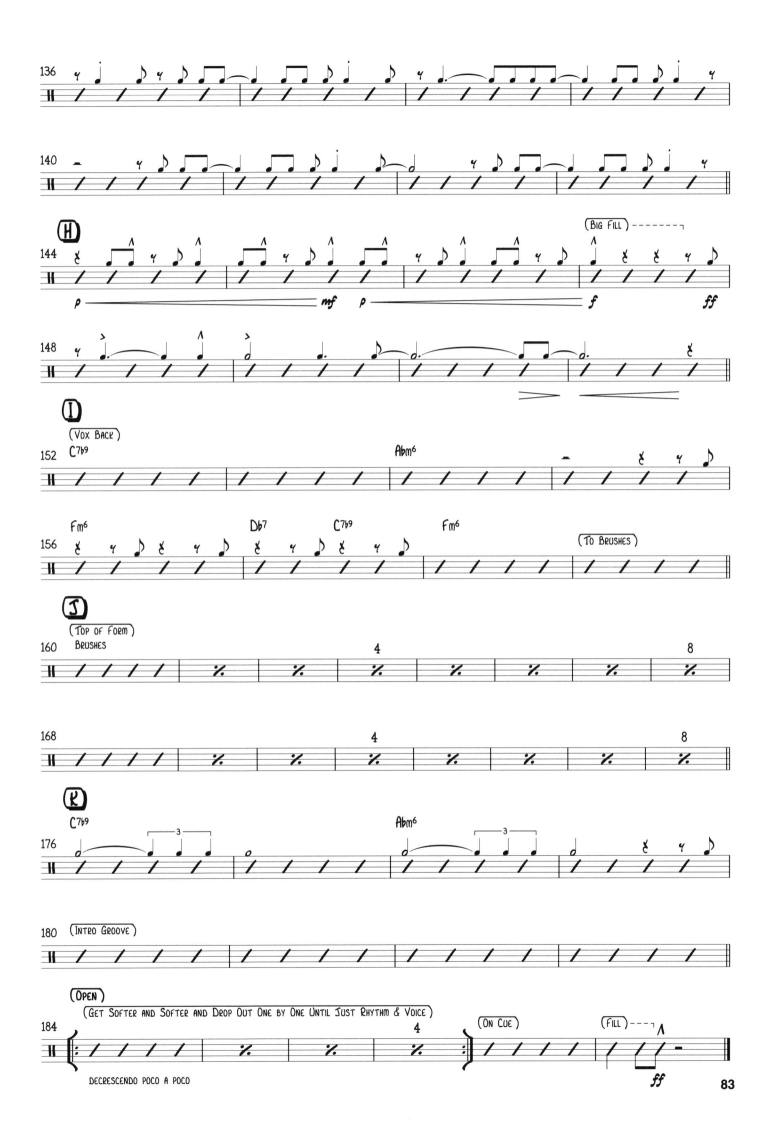

DECRESCENDO POCO A POCO

"Soul Conversations" (Straight Eighths)

Composers: Ulysses Owens Jr., Takeshi Ohbayashi

Arranger: Danny Jonokuchi

Reference Recording

Ulysses Owens Jr. Big Band, *Soul Conversations*

New Century Jazz Quintet, *Soul Conversions*

Performance Notes

The consistency of the brush groove for this tune is my motivation. The goal here is to maintain the pattern and groove and, again, to not overplay in the typical big band fashion.

Drums

SOUL CONVERSATION

Composed by Ulysses Owens Jr. and Takeshi Ohbayashi
Arranged by Danny Jonokuchi

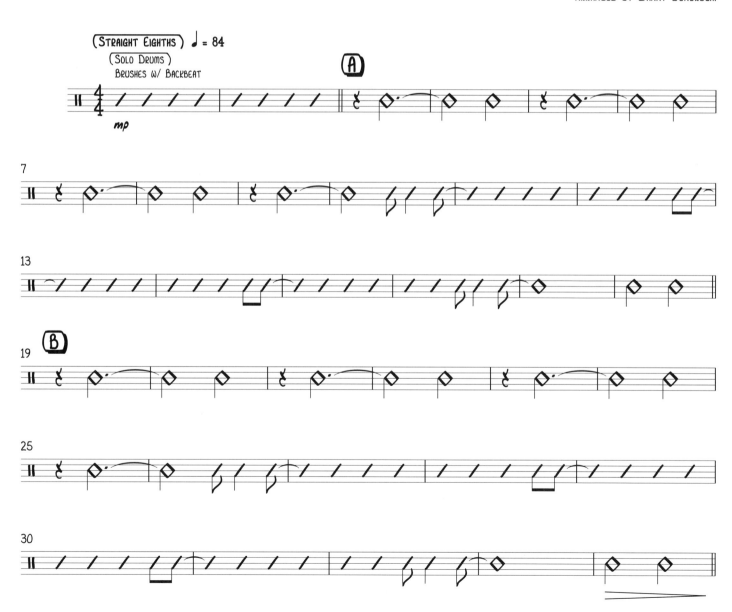

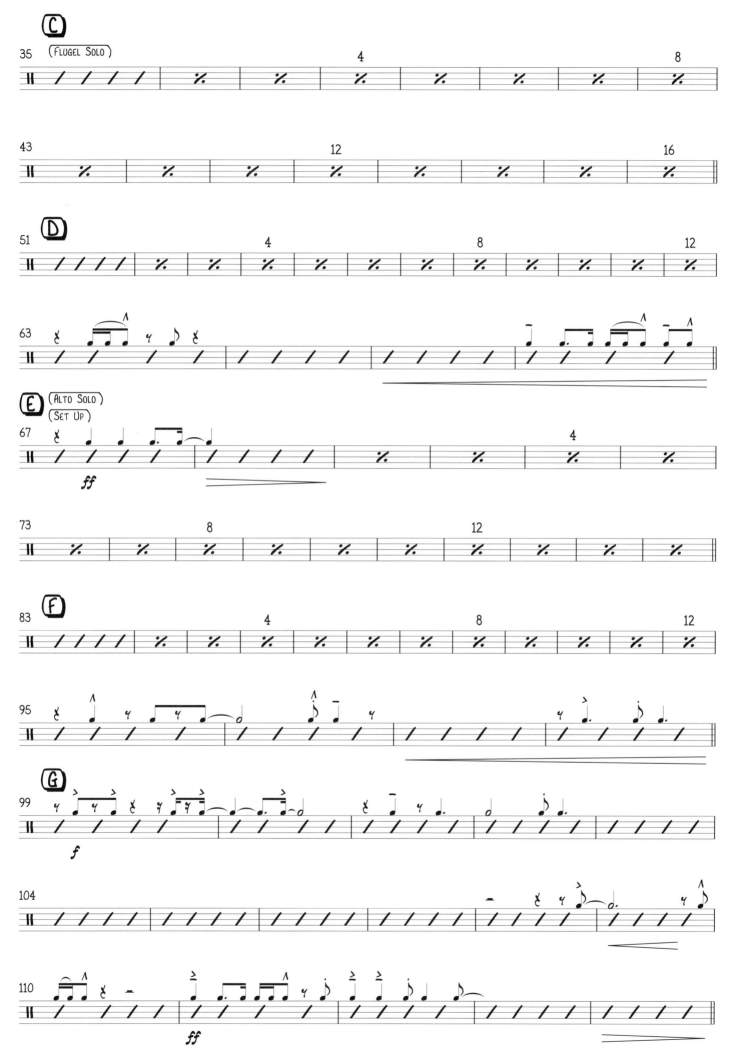

"Nature Boy" (Latin/Straight Eighths)

Composer: Eden Ahbez

Arrangers: Peter Tijerina, Michael Dease

Reference Recordings

Ulysses Owens Jr. Big Band, "Nature Boy"

Kurt Elling, *The Messenger*

Performance Notes

This composition is a big tune, and it requires a strong groove from the drummer. The core groove was derived from Kurt Elling's arrangement penned by Laurence Hobgood. Check out that version, coupled with my big band arrangement.

Drums

Nature Boy

Eden Ahbez
Arranged by Peter Tijerina and Michael Dease

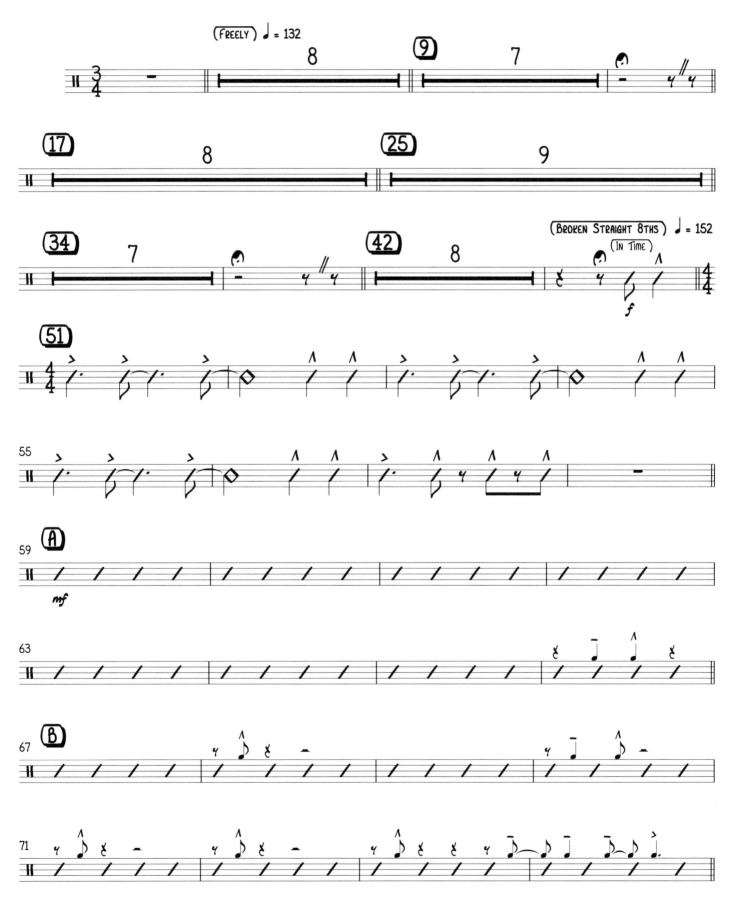

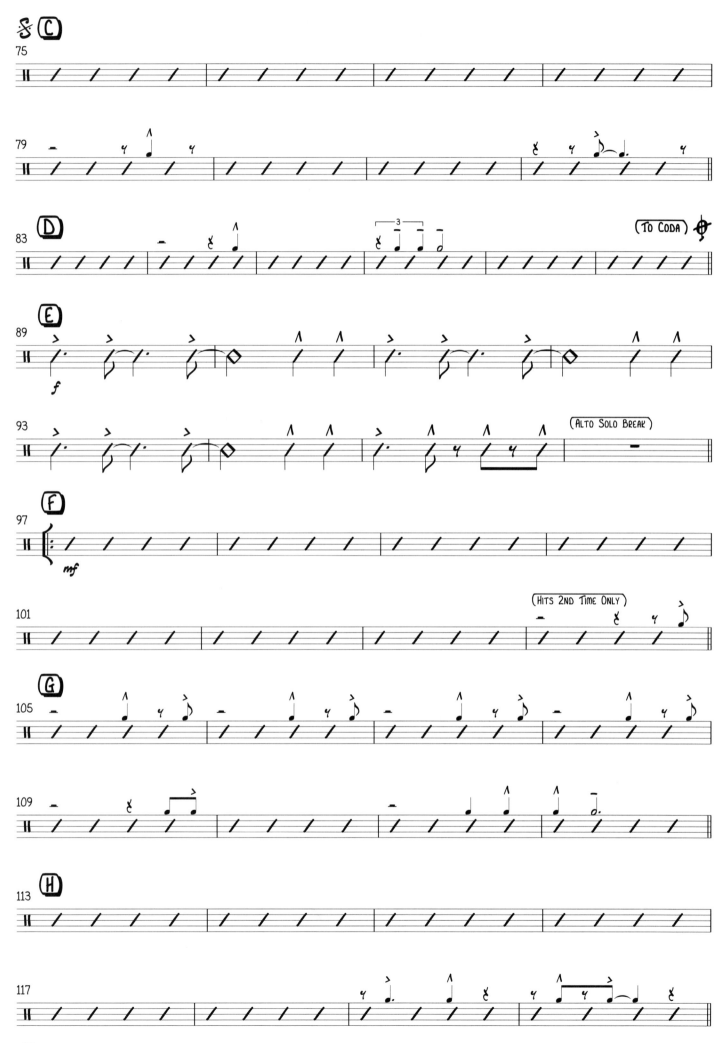

"What's Going On" (Funk)

Composer: Marvin Gaye, Al Cleveland, Renaldo Benson

Arranger: Diego Rivera

Reference Recording

Ulysses Owens Jr. Big Band

Performance Notes

Diego Rivera is one of my favorite big band arrangers. This is because he understands how to write to the core of the sound of my band, and this tune is my favorite. It's based on Marvin Gaye's tune, "What's Going On," and the key is to approach the groove from the same place as the legendary Chet Forest.

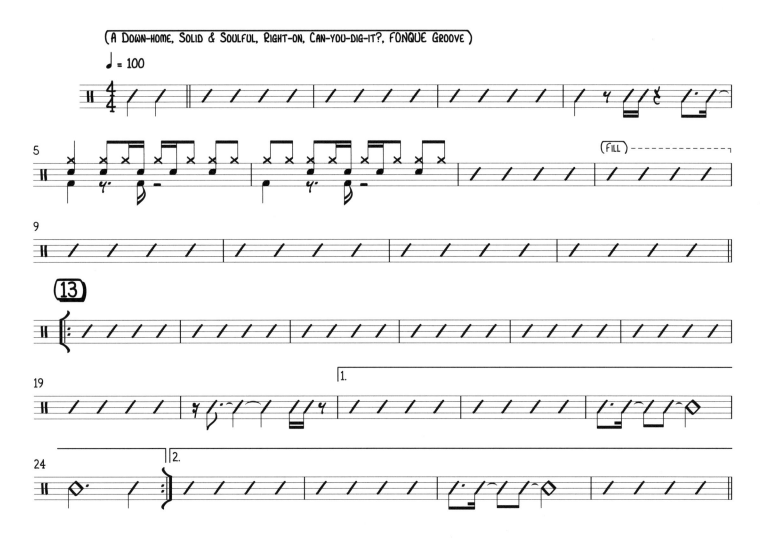

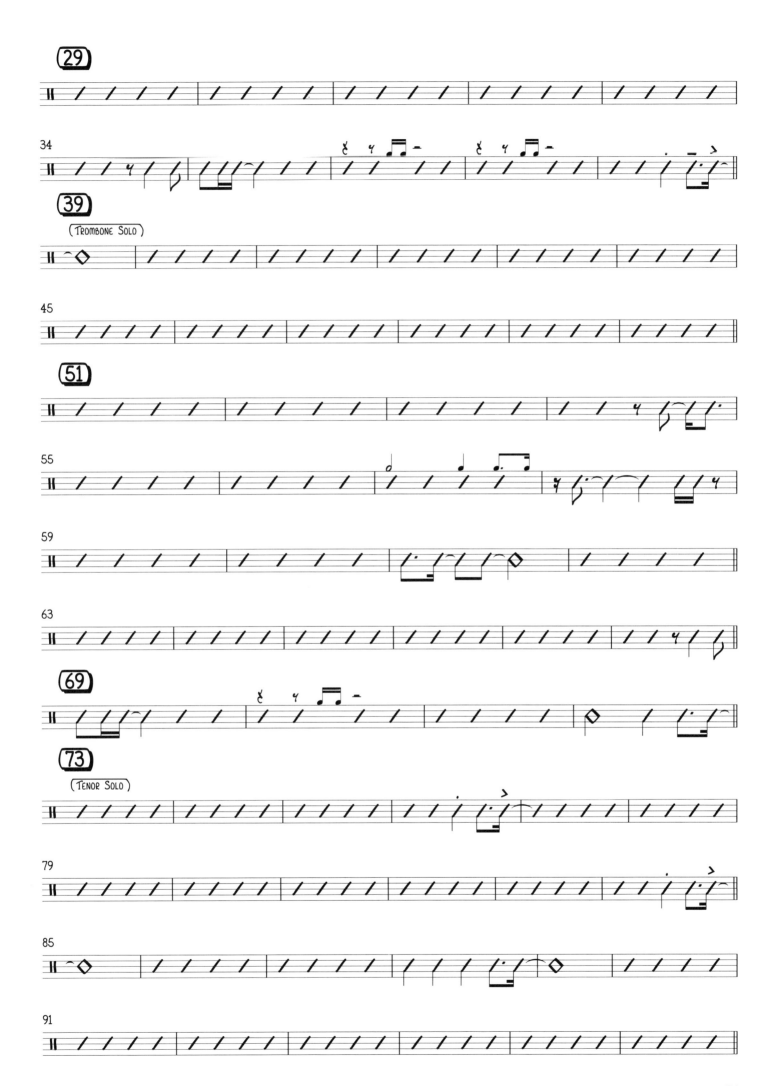

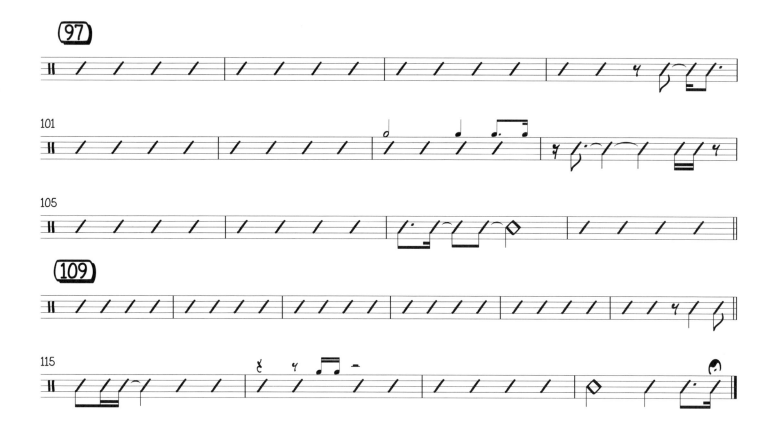

"Good and Terrible" (Odd Meter)

Composer: Michael Dease

Arranger: J. Hainsworth

Reference Recording

Ulysses Owens Jr., *Unanimous*

Performance Notes

The first recording of this tune is on my album *Unanimous*. It's a quintet recording, and my approach is very driving, almost like a straight-eighth tune but in 5/4. The key within the big band version of this tune is to have that same drive and pulse but to catch the hits without the groove being broken up.

Drums

Good and Terrible

Music by Michael Dease
Arranged by J. Hainsworth

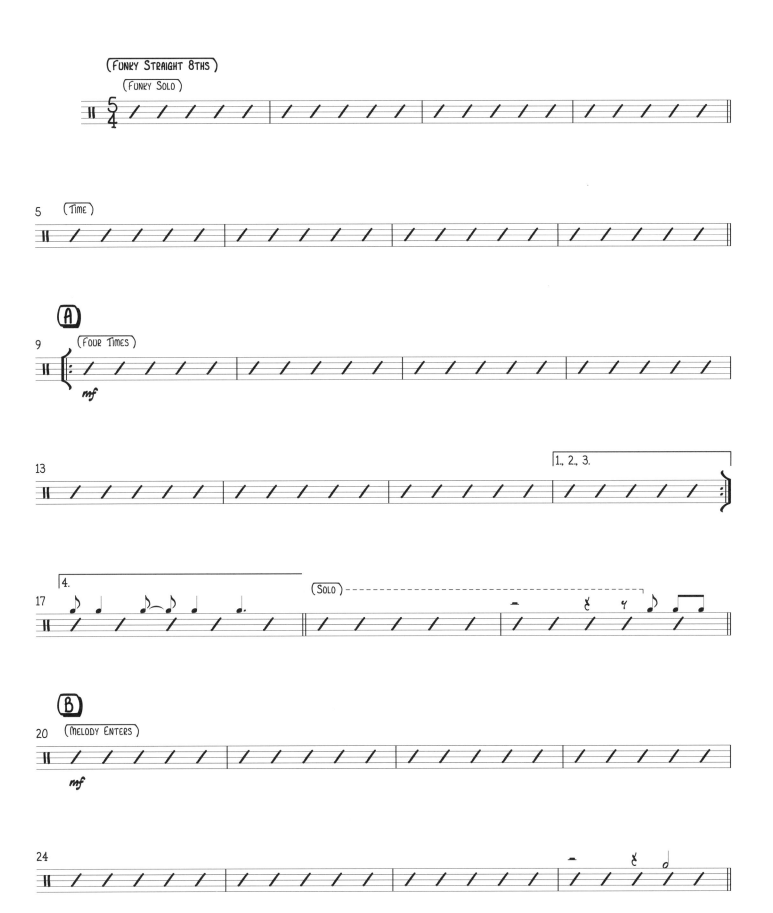

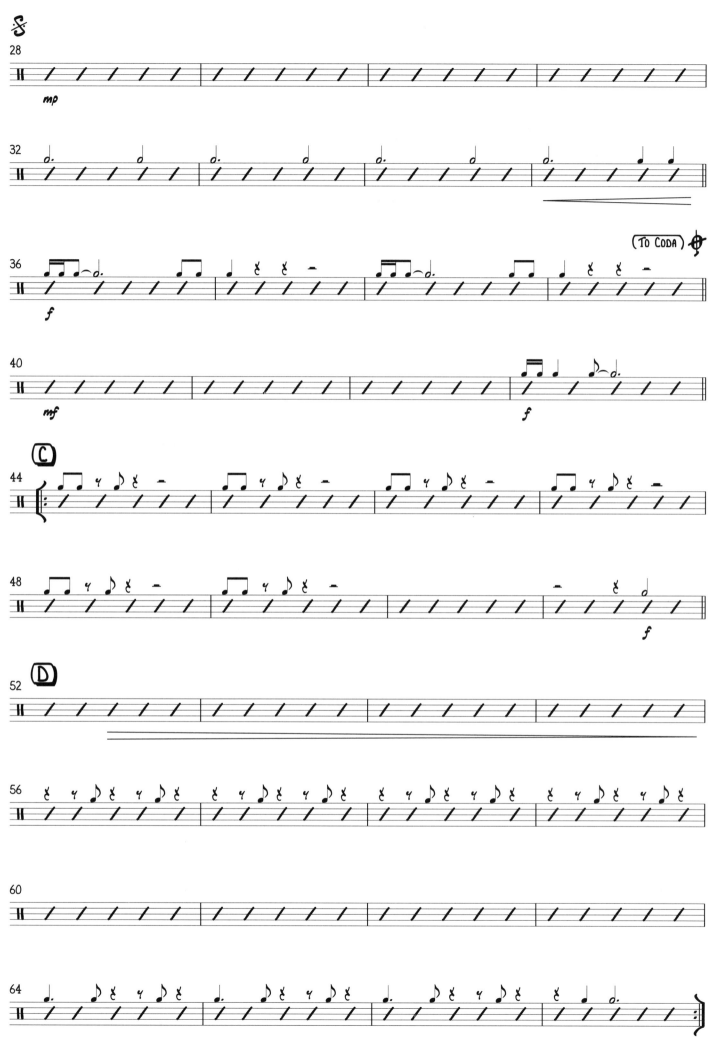

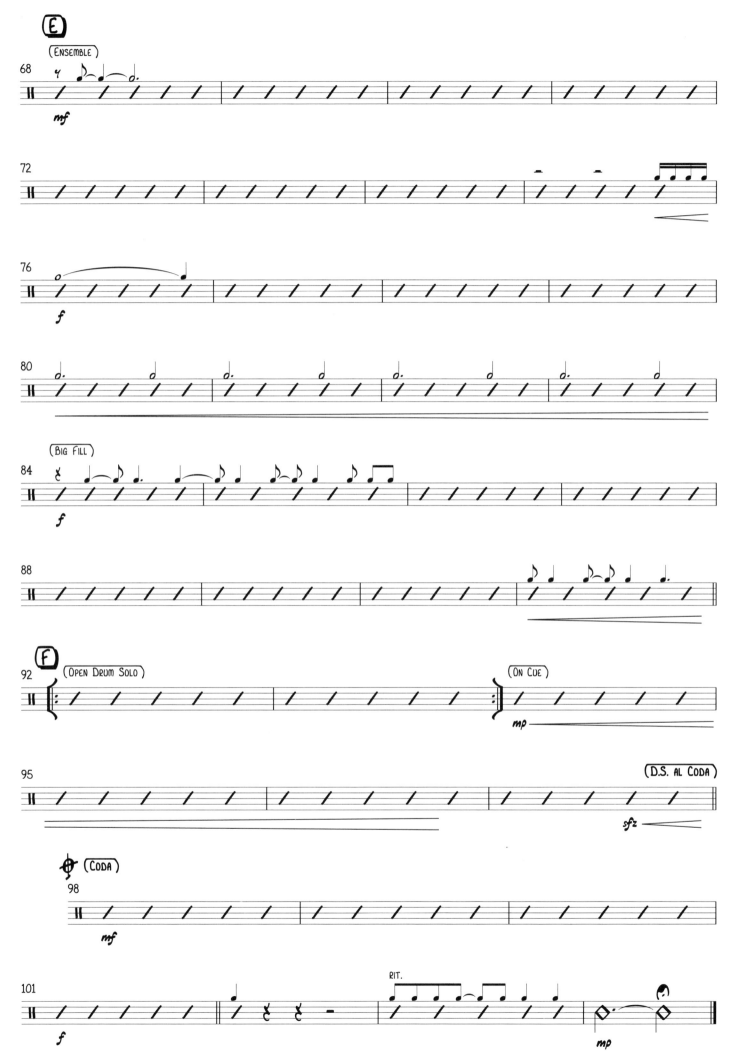

"Blame It on My Youth" (Vocal Ballad)

Composer: Oscar Levant

Arranger: Danny Jonokuchi

Reference Recording

Danny Jonokuchi Big Band, *Voices*

Performance Notes

Something to consider when performing this chart is that it's a vocal chart, which requires a dynamic level of playing that supports the band but does not overshadow the vocalist. It's a pretty standard feeling chart, but pay attention to the hits within the music that require shaping and those through which you can just simply play time.

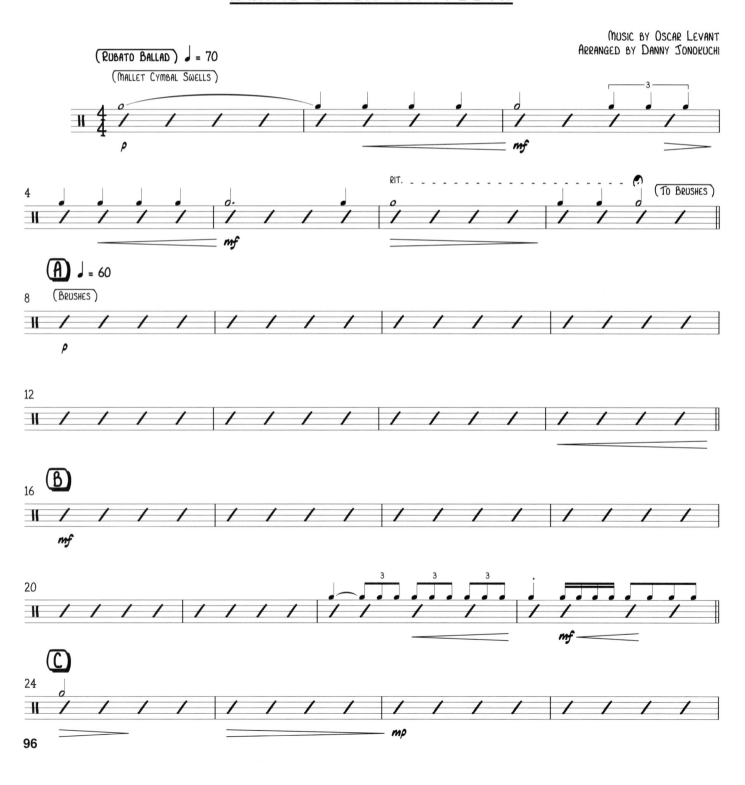

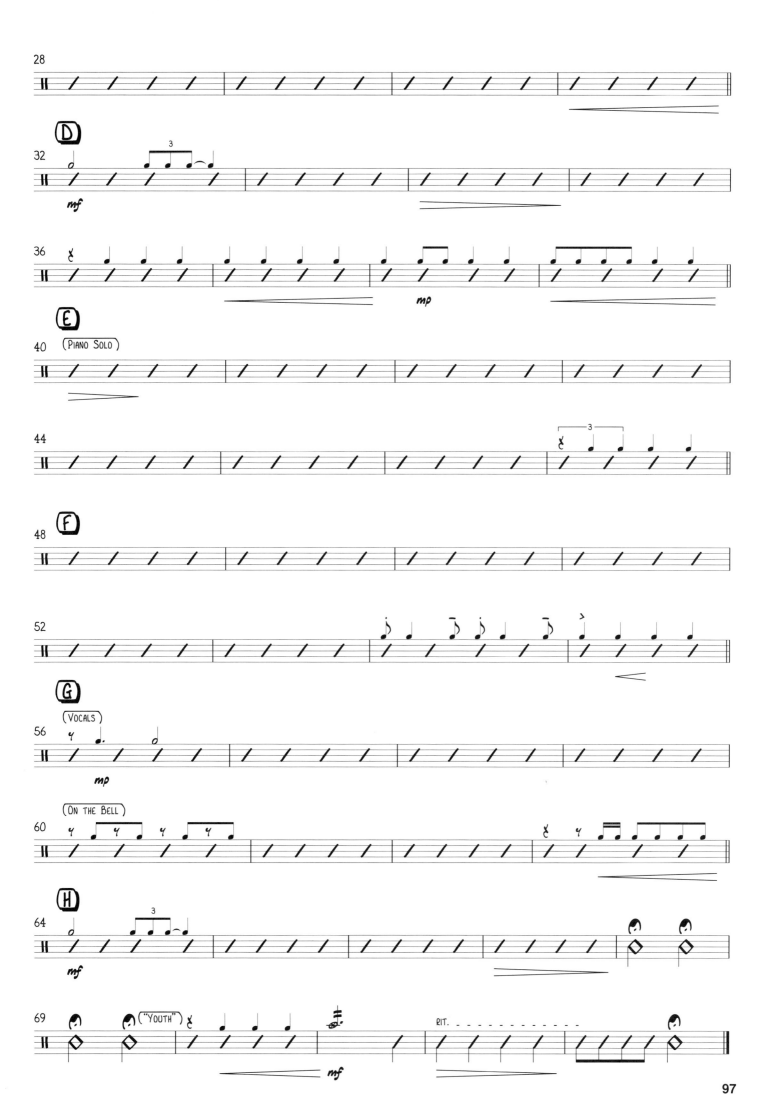

"Like Someone in Love" (Uptempo Swing)

Composer: Jimmy Van Heusen

Arranger: Danny Jonokuchi

Reference Recording

Danny Jonokuchi Big Band

Performance Notes

This chart is a medium swing chart in the modern style, which requires a lot of orchestrating. The first thing to check out is the intro; be careful not to overplay the hits while still following through with the big hits, keeping the groove steady. I really like this chart because it's a blend of traditional and modern swing, and it's very much in the style of the Thad Jones and Mel Lewis Orchestra.

Like Someone in Love

Music by Jimmy Van Heusen
Arranged by Danny Jonokuchi

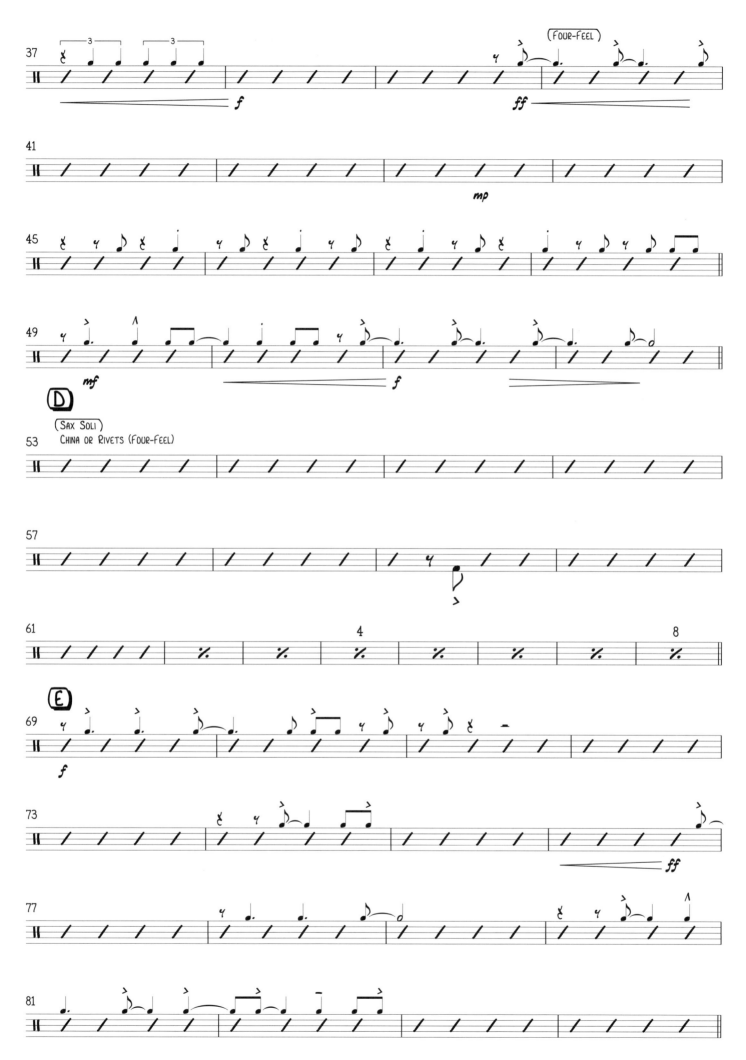

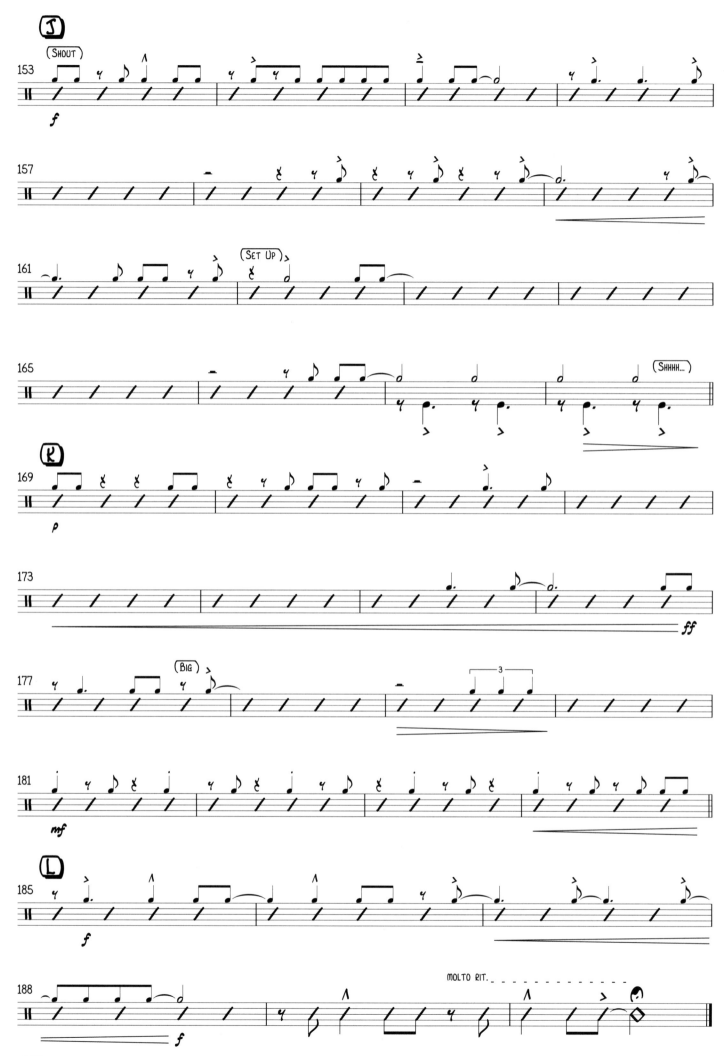

Part 6: Time to Gig

This book was created for every drummer to learn essential information and then gig with any big band all across the country and world. I feel that the ultimate affirmation for a musician is to have the ability to perform with a band, and it's the whole goal of all these exercises and the experiences that you will gain.

CHAPTER 16: Choosing the Right Gear

A major part of big band drumming is having the right gear. This chapter is not designed for you to stress your financial budget or to think that by having the right gear, you will automatically get gigs. However, for big band, you must utilize the right tools to have the maximum impact. As a small ensemble drummer, your personality is identifiable through your cymbal and drum selection. As a big band drummer, your personality isn't as important as your ability to cut through the band and hold it together.

To me, bigger drums tuned low is something that applies well in the big band context. Below is a general set-up that has worked well for me throughout my big band career.

The Big Band Drum Kit

Big Band Drums

Typically, when it comes to big band, I use bigger drums, and these are sizes I prefer. (I usually use Tama Star maple or walnut drums.)

20" x 16" Bass Drum

16" x 16" Floor Tom

14" x 14" Floor Tom

12" x 8" Tom

14" x 5 1/2" or 14" x 6" Snare Drum

Big Band Cymbals

I use brighter cymbals with a big band as opposed to darker cymbals.

22" Ride Cymbal (Avedis Series or Brighter Series)

20" Crash (K Light Crash, Avedis A Crash)

18" Crash (K Light Crash, Avedis Crash)

19" Extreme K Crash or 20" A Custom China Cymbal with Rivets

14" Hi-Hats (Avedis or New Beat)

The Right Sticks

When it comes to drumsticks, feel free to mix and match the types of materials used for the tips; you'll find that some materials work better for cymbals and others work better for drumheads.

Promark 7A Rebound Wood Tip (Left Hand)

7A Nylon (Right Hand)

Drumheads

I use Evans G1 or UV1 coated drumheads on all toms and snares. For the bass drum, I use a coated UV1 or a Calftone bass drumhead (EMad) so that I have some punch. Place the Evans muffling system on the inside of the bass drum to deaden the sound a bit. This is so you can have a nice low end present in the bass drum, which is necessary for big band.

Tuning

It's helpful to reference great drummers and their tuning as a guide for your own playing. For me, I take my cue from drummers like Herlin Riley, Dennis Mackrel, Buddy Rich, and even Mel Lewis for how I desire the drums to feel and sound within the big band.

Snare: Medium tension, but still able to crack through the band

High Tom: Tuned higher

Floor Toms: Tuned lower

Bass Drum: Punchy with some low end

On the Road

When on the road, I don't have the ability to take my kit, so I'll give some size options that I'll accept that will help me get the job done. I've categorized them into two groups.

Set-Up 1
    22" x 16" Bass Drum
    16" x 16" Floor Tom
    12" x 8" Tom
    14" x 5 1/2" Snare Drum

Set-Up 2
    20" x 16" Bass Drum
    16" x 16" Floor Tom
    14" x 14" Floor Tom
    10" x 7" Tom
    14" x 6" Snare Drum

CHAPTER 17: Auditioning for Ensembles

Auditioning for ensembles is something you'll run into when working as a jazz drummer. The key to a successful audition is preparation and making sure that you are aware of what is required for each opportunity. Within each section below, I've listed things you have to prepare for as a drummer to excel in each audition and secure the job/performance opportunity.

Types of Ensemble Scenarios

Below are several situations that you may find yourself in, particularly if you're a younger player.

Auditioning for High School Big Band

My first experience with big band was in high school, and I was selected for the Jazz 1 Ensemble in ninth grade even though I had limited jazz ensemble playing experience.

What I had, based on my ability to play in church, was knowing how to keep a groove solid and make it feel good, even if my familiarity with the knowledge of the groove in jazz wasn't strong. I was also not afraid to speak up if I didn't know the groove, and the instructor or auditioning faculty taught it to me right on the spot.

For high school band ensembles, this is what is required:

- Proficiency in playing swing, shuffle, funk, rock, Afro-Cuban, ballad, and New Orleans grooves with confidence.

- Remain teachable and be able to adjust quickly to whatever the director requests.

- Be able to play with confidence and the right volume level while keeping things solid for the band.

- Learn to read music, which for me began with classical piano lessons at the age of eight. I recommend this to all musicians, especially if you primarily play drums. This teaches you the basic functions of music (form, melody, harmony, rhythm) and how to recognize them, along with reading sheet music.

- Study the charts and memorize them so that you can cue the band without disrupting the groove.

- Keep your ears open and be able to play concise fills and solos that are helpful to the band.

Auditioning for High School All District and All State

When auditioning, look at the audition excerpts and study them with a teacher who has been successful at that as well. Most of the adjudication panels are looking for musicians that can play the excerpts with proficiency and not in a robotic manner. Practice creating musicality with the excerpts while also playing the rhythms verbatim. Most of the auditioning faculty are looking for your attention to detail because once you are placed in those ensembles, you must be able to play the selected repertoire.

Auditioning for College Ensembles

There are tons of college big bands, and many of the directors desire the same things discussed in the high school ensemble section. If you have an opportunity to hear the big band you are auditioning for, then go for it—everything helps. Also, seek to take a lesson with the faculty drum instructor of the college so they can assess your skill and see if you would be a good fit for the program.

Essentially Ellington

Duke Ellington charts must be played a certain way, and if you have never listened to Sonny Greer, or any number of Ellington drummers, it will be challenging to play these charts with the right feeling. Plus, there is a long history of drummers who have played this music well, so studying the sound of Duke Ellington's band will be key.

Grammy Band

The Grammy Band is an opportunity for high school students to audition and be part of this educational program, launched by the National Recording Academy.

Jack Rudin Competition

Jazz at Lincoln Center hosts an annual competition for college bands. This is more of an ensemble competition, so the key is making sure that you adhere to the vision and sound that your director has set.

Broadway and Show Drumming

Another element of big band drumming exists within the context of Broadway and shows that are primarily for entertainment. It's important to study that genre of drumming and perfect it. A great resource for this kind of drumming is a book by the great Ed Shaughnessy called *Show Drumming: The Essential Guide to Playing Drumset for Live Shows and Musicals* (Hal Leonard), which speaks in greater detail about how to show up prepared and get the job. I have a fair amount of experience on Broadway with shows like *Cotton Club Parade*, which is a heavy, Ellington-based show. Key elements in show drumming are playing with excellent metronomic time, reading the chart correctly, and being consistent.

I played *Cotton Club Parade* about 25 to 30 times, and each time, there was no room for error because so many dance and speaking cues were connected to my role as the drummer. I think every drummer should play for an off-Broadway or touring musical show because it really helps you understand the core of what makes the drummer necessary in the music as a time-keeper.

CHAPTER 18: Recording with a Big Band

Recording with a big band is challenging. I remember listening to the playbacks during a recording session with the Christian McBride Big Band, and from that exercise, I started playing much differently. I started playing based on how to make the band sound good from a listener's perspective, not a drummer's perspective.

Working in the Studio

Here are some keys to creating a solid recording with a big band.

Recording Set-Up

I have received a few amazing opportunities to record with some high-profile big bands, and one of my favorites was with the John Beasley Monk'estra and the late, great Al Schmitt engineering at Capitol Studios in Los Angeles. Thankfully, I have a relationship with Tama Drums, and they supplied an incredible kit for me. I was able to arrive at the studio early and get the drums tuned up and feeling great. It's important with the studio, especially at high-profile sessions, to get there super early so that you have time to go through your process. Also, bring moon gels, gaff tape, and any other dampening materials so that whatever the bandleader and engineer requires of you, you are able to produce.

Working with the Engineer

I have been fortunate to work with some of the best recording engineers in the jazz industry, including Joe Ferla, Al Schmitt, Dave Darlington, Todd Whitelock, Chris Allen, and many others. What they all share is that they have their own preference for how they like to capture the drums, but they will be sensitive to your needs as well. All of them are very flexible with microphone heights, making sure your ability to make music is not impeded. But you must trust them to do their job, as they trust you to do your job; make sure you respect them and what they ask of you. Recording is a different beast than playing live, and it requires different things than what you may be accustomed to.

Lock in the Groove

The primary goal of the drummer is to play the groove and keep the time solid. The first thing you should work on is locking in with the bass player and pianist, making sure the groove is solid.

Catch the Hits

This is crucial for recordings because if you miss a hit while recording, it lives there forever! So catching all of the hits with the brass will assist you in achieving a solid recording.

Dynamics

Playing dynamics will shift the band to a mature sonic experience, which is the most powerful thing about great big band drummers. They have the power to make the band play as soft as a whisper and as thunderous as lightning!

Drum and Cymbal Sounds

This is really important because if you play cymbals that are too dry and small, it won't cut through the band. If the drums are small sizes, they won't resonate with the band and give them something to hold on to. I prefer to use a 20" bass drum, 14" x 14" and 16" x 16" floor toms, a 12" x 8" tom, and a 5 1/2" x 14" or 6" x 14" snare drum that can crack through the band.

Microphone Placement

Hire a great engineer, because if you are playing all the right stuff and it's not recorded, then it won't work. Microphone quality and placement is key. It's important to make sure the engineer places the right microphone in the right position on the drums. I have a diagram of a good template for microphone placement on the following page.

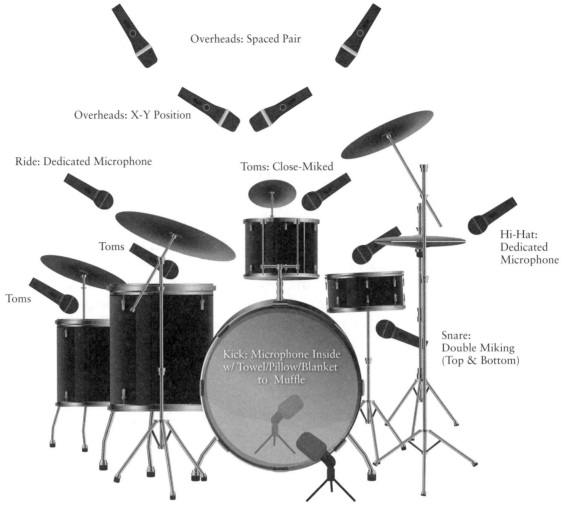

Overheads: Spaced Pair

Overheads: X-Y Position

Ride: Dedicated Microphone

Toms: Close-Miked

Hi-Hat: Dedicated Microphone

Toms

Toms

Kick: Microphone Inside w/ Towel/Pillow/Blanket to Muffle

Snare: Double Miking (Top & Bottom)

Kick: Additional Microphone Outside (Front)

Drum Studio Isolation

I was called in to handle post-production on a project, and the drums were recorded in the live room with the horns. It was a nightmare, so please never make this mistake! When recording the big band, drums should be isolated from everyone else in the band; otherwise, it won't be a clean recording.

Live Recording

My album *Soul Conversations* was recorded live at Dizzy's Club Coca-Cola in New York City at Jazz at Lincoln Center. Thankfully, I was working with Rob Macomber, who is great and skilled at live recording. However, baffles had to be placed between myself and the bass player who was behind me, to make sure our instruments were recorded cleanly.

Editing/Mixing/Mastering

Another element of my talent and skillset is my production ability, and many times in recording, I am tuning into certain things as a player because I am fully aware of what the editing, mixing, and mastering engineer is going to have to deal with. Learning your music will make their lives easier.

Drumheads/Muffling/Tuning

It's important to approach the drums with the right head textures and muffling. Here are some muffling options for the drums and devices that are helpful.

- For snare drum and tom muffling, I like to use R-Tom moon gels, and, depending on the sound you are trying to achieve, you can decide how many you want to utilize on each drum.

- For the bass drum, I like to use an Evans bass drum pad inside of the bass drum, which gives it a punchy sound.

CHAPTER 19: Playing the Gig

There is an unspoken set of rules that comes with playing a gig that all professional musicians are aware of, and I want you to end the book being fully aware of them.

1. **Be on time to the gig:** Occasionally, there are challenges that can impede you from being on time, but if you have a great record, then people will know it's a special scenario that is keeping you from being on time.

2. **Be focused and present at the gig:** No one wants to work with a musician who is unfocused. There is always another musician who is ready and able to play the gig, and be fully available for the gig.

3. **Equipment:** As stated earlier, have all the necessary equipment that you need to fulfill the gig to the best of your ability.

4. **Practice the music:** If you can, run through the charts ahead of time. For big bands, this is really key to playing the music and also getting a head start on learning everyone else's part.

5. **Lock in with the bandleader:** They will need your compliance with their vision for the band. I have already stated that the drummer is the unofficial conductor, but the bandleader might be the arranger or composer, and you have to respect their vision within your role as the driving force of the band.

6. **Be a fun person to work with:** No one likes to work with a jerk!

7. **Have fun:** The band is able to be either great or terrible with you; give them a great experience.

Amateur Talent vs. Mastery

When drummers ask me why I chose to write about big band drumming or jazz brushes (the subject of my other book), they also ask why those topics are relevant. What's interesting to me is my question back to them: "When did they no longer become relevant?" It's something to think about...

I remember when I started playing drums around the age of two; I was first taught a funk groove. Then, when I started taking drum lessons, I was taught Latin, rock, and more intricate funk grooves. Later on, when I joined the high school big band, I learned how to swing and play brushes. This was part of the natural progression of mastering my instrument.

My challenge to you is that if you want to continue on the journey of mastery, big band drumming is a natural part of that journey. Otherwise, you will be an incomplete musician who only knows how to play one style. For my playing, the better I was able to understand other styles and genres, the more respect I had towards the genre that I chose to focus on, which is jazz.

In this new generation, I find that a lot of musicians are seeking success and not mastery. However, many of the greatest artists that we still speak about were masters, and mastery will never be duplicated or rivaled. My encouragement to all of you is to take the journey of mastery, and it will set you apart from the other musicians, creating a great space for you in the world of drumming and beyond.

Happy swingin',

U

ACKNOWLEDGMENTS

The idea for this book derived from my years of playing with various big bands since I started as a 14-year-old student at Douglas Anderson School of the Arts with the Jazz 1 band under the direction of Ace Martin. I am grateful to Ace Martin who taught me, within four years, most of what I needed to understand from a foundational perspective on how to support a big band. The first "big band" I ever played with was my church choir, and I owe much to Kevin Sibley, Elwyn "Hugh" Currington, and Elijah "Gene" Demps for teaching me how to support them musically.

Ricky Kirkland was the first great big band drummer I saw play. I am so grateful he was my first jazz drum instructor, and I will forever sing his praises. John Riley was the first famous drummer I saw play with the Vanguard Jazz Orchestra at the University of North Florida, and his playing became part of what I aspire towards as a big band drummer.

Herlin Riley, you will forever be the "cat" for me in terms of how to play with a big band. What you accomplished with the Lincoln Center Jazz Orchestra will forever be etched into our musical minds. The bar was set with your playing and approach.

Victor Goines, at times I simply thought you did not like my drumming because you were so hard on me, but I later realized you were my biggest fan and you understood my potential. Thank you for educating me on how to be a proficient big band drummer.

Juilliard Jazz Orchestra conductors Arturo O'Farrill, Bob Stewart, Loren Schoenberg, and Wycliffe Gordon, thank you for laying the foundation for me.

Barry Cooper, thank you for introducing my name to Butch Miles and making it possible for me to get the call to play with the greatest big band in the land, the Count Basie Orchestra. Butch Miles, thanks for believing in me.

Christian McBride, thanks for giving me the opportunity to create a sound that became your Grammy-winning big band, and I will forever be grateful. Keep winning Grammys, but remember, we won the first one together. #TheGoodFeeling :)

Michael Dease, thanks for helping me to start my own big band and to always dream bigger for my career than I sometimes have the capacity to think of.

Zack Olsen, you are my right hand in writing drum books, and I refuse to create one without you. You single-handedly helped me to focus this book and create a resource for a generation of drummers that need to understand this art form of playing in the big band.

Thanks to my family for your support during the time of writing this book: Mom, Dad, Felicia, Iris, and Kyler (B3). Love to you all and thanks for being my motivation. Jocelyn, thanks for your love and support during this crazy time seeking to write a book coupled with the other million things that I have going on daily; yet your love never waivers towards me.

Myles, Rory, and Lorraine, thank you for your support always within my career. #UnlimitedMyles

To all of the big bands I have been fortunate to work with: You are the reason I have the ability to write this book.

Juilliard Jazz Orchestra, Jazz Museum in Harlem All Stars, Christian McBride Big Band, Kurt Elling, John Clayton, Count Basie Orchestra, Michael Dease Big Band, Steven Feifke Big Band, John Beasley Monk'estra, and Ulysses Owens Jr. Big Band: THANK YOU!

Jeff Schroedl, I appreciate you always believing in me and my writing!

To every drummer who reads this book, I hope it assists you in becoming the drummer that big bands and the world needs! Keep in touch and let me know how this book helps you; tag me in your practice routines and sessions.

www.UlyssesOwensJr.com
Instagram: UlyssesOwensJr.
Facebook: Ulysses Owens Jr.

Book Team

Book Concept Consultant: Zack Olsen
Book Proofreader: Megan Rickman
Book Cover Photo: Felicia Bass
Book Cover Design: Hal Leonard
Notation: Zachary Adelman and Zack Olsen
Transcription: Zachary Adelman
Mixing/Mastering Engineer: Liston Gregory III
Recording Engineer: Ulysses Owens Jr. at UOJ Productions Studio, Jacksonville, FL

Big Band Arrangers:
Danny Jonokuchi
Diego Rivera
Jason Hainsworth
Michael Dease
Michael Thomas
Steven Feifke

All Ulysses Owens Jr. Big Band charts come from the album *Soul Conversations* under the Outside In music label

Ulysses Owens Jr. Big Band

Walter Andre Cano, Trumpet 1
Benny Benack III, Trumpet 2
Summer Camargo, Trumpet 3
Giveton Gelin, Trumpet 4
Alexa Tarantino, Alto Sax 1
Erena Terakubo, Alto Sax 2
Diego Rivera, Tenor Sax 1
Daniel Dickinson, Tenor Sax 2
Andrew Gutauskas, Bari Sax

Michael Dease, Trombone 1
Chris Glassman, Sub Trombone 2
Eric Miller, Trombone 2
Gina Benalcazar, Trombone 3
Wyatt Forhan, Bass Trombone
Takeshi Ohbayashi, Piano
Yasushi Nakamura, Bass
Stefon Harris, Vibes
Charles Turner, Vocal

ABOUT THE AUTHOR

Three-time Grammy Award-winning drummer Ulysses Owens Jr. is known for being a drummer who *The New York Times* has said "take[s] a back seat to no one" and is "a musician who balances excitement gracefully and shines with innovation."

Performer, producer, and educator Ulysses Owens Jr. goes the limit in the jazz world and beyond, claiming eight successful albums of his own. Owens has also gained special attention for his performances on Grammy Award-winning albums by Kurt Elling and the Christian McBride Big Band. On February 3rd, 2023, he received his third Grammy Award for his participation on the album *Generation Gap Jazz Orchestra* featuring Steven Feifke and Bijon Watson. In addition to his awards, he has also performed on five Grammy Award-nominated albums with artists such as Joey Alexander, Christian McBride Trio, John Beasley's Monk'estra, and Gregory Porter.

Both *Jazziz* and *Rolling Stone* magazines picked his album *Songs of Freedom* as a Top Ten Album for 2019; in 2021, his most recent big band release, *Soul Conversations*, was voted Top Album in May 2021 by *Jazziz* magazine. *Soul Conversations* received rave reviews and was added to multiple playlists on Apple Music, Spotify, and Sirius XM, and now the band is touring nationally. The Ulysses Owens Jr. Big Band has also been voted "Rising Star Big Band" of 2022 by *Downbeat* magazine.

His upcoming eighth album release, *A New Beat*, will feature his new "Generation Y" Band on the Cellar Music record label. The album was produced by Jeremy Pelt and recorded at the legendary Van Gelder Studio in New Jersey.

As an author, Ulysses has published two books, *Jazz Brushes for the Modern Drummer: An Essential Guide to the Art of Keeping Time* (Hal Leonard) and *The Musician's Career Guide: Turning Your Talent into Sustained Success* (distributed by Simon and Schuster). His third book, *Jazz Big Band for the Modern Drummer: An Essential Guide to Supporting the Large Jazz Ensemble*, also for Hal Leonard, will be released in January 2024. He is also a regular contributing writer for the WJCT Jacksonville Music Experience, *Downbeat* magazine, *Jazz Times* magazine, *Percussive Notes* (official journal of the Percussive Arts Society), and an op-ed contributor for the *Florida Times-Union* newspaper.

As an educator, Ulysses has been a part of the jazz faculty at the Juilliard School as Small Ensemble Director for over seven years and has served on the EDIB (Equity, Diversity, Inclusion, and Belonging) committee. He has also served on multiple panels and taught various workshops within the Alan D. Marks Entrepreneurship division. He is the Artistic Director for his family's non-profit arts organization, Don't Miss a Beat, and the newly appointed Artistic Director for the Friday Musicale Summer Jazz Camp in Jacksonville, FL. Ulysses is currently serving a three-year appointment as the Educational Artist in Residence for SF Performances in San Francisco, CA, where he specializes in community outreach and gives workshops across the Bay Area in San Francisco and in the Oakland public school system and music programs.

Ulysses is also the creator of multiple online jazz drum video courses: "Finding Your Beat," "The Art of Swing," and "Jazz Drumming 101: Everything You Need to Know to Get the Gig," for the Open Studio online platform. He has also hosted the highly successful weekly live YouTube series "From the Drummer's Perspective." Recently, Owens was asked to join the Drumeo online educational platform as their Inaugural Jazz Drum Instructor. With Drumeo, he is developing the curriculum for his interactive course "30 Days to Becoming a Jazz Drummer," that will launch in June 2024.

As a cultural entrepreneur, Ulysses has been awarded the Difference Maker award from Beacon College, the Robert Arleigh White Award for Advocacy from the Cultural Council of Northeast Florida, and has been a multi-year recipient of the Individual Artist Grant from the Community Foundation for Northeast Florida. He was also honored with the 2023 Ann McDonald Baker Art Ventures Award from the Community Foundation for Northeast Florida, selected as "40 Under 40" by *Jacksonville Business Journal* in 2022, and is part of the 2023 Leadership Jacksonville class.

He remains consistently in demand for new projects and consulting opportunities as one of the most sought-after thought-leaders of his generation. Yet, what matters to him consistently is giving back and continuing to be grateful for a new day to make a difference in the lives of others.

Ulysses received his Bachelor of Fine Arts from the Juilliard School in 2006 and was the first African-American jazz drummer to be admitted to their Inaugural Jazz Program in 2001.